MAHATMA
A SCIENTIST OF
THE INTUITIVELY OBVIOUS

Promod Kumar Sharma

PARTRIDGE
A Penguin Random House Company

To order additional copies of this book, contact
Partridge India
000 800 10062 62
www.partridgepublishing.com/india
orders.india@partridgepublishing.com

CONTENTS

AUTHOR'S SUBMISSION

Gandhi was not a politician. Gandhi was not a philosopher. Gandhi was not a visionary. Gandhi was not a spiritual leader. Gandhi did not have a practical approach to any issue. Gandhi was an obstinate old man who did not listen to any body. Gandhi contributed little in making the country free from British rule. Gandhi could not prevent division of India. These are the remarks I come across about Gandhi from some of his critics in India.

Aren't these remarks somewhat violent? Gandhi said, "The only answer to violence is non-violence." I thought I should follow what Gandhi said; therefore I decided to write this book.

Notwithstanding the remarks given above, the saintly thinker and poet Ravindra Nath Tagore called him Mahatma. Netaji Subhash Chandra Bose, one of Gandhi's distinguished followers, who disagreed with Gandhi's philosophy of non-violence and formed an army to fight British with arms; called him Rashtra Pita (Father of the Nation). Crores of people from India who lovingly called him Bapu (father) cried in deep anguish and could not take their meals on the day when their "Bapu" died on the 30th of January in 1948.

When India sensed that British Raj would ultimately end, the nation rejoiced, but Gandhi felt lonely. He thought true freedom for its people was still far away.

A lot has been said and written about Mahatma Gandhi by highly learned and distinguished authors, philosophers, politicians and intellectuals of all shades. It is beyond me to add to the existing information available about Gandhi. I am, therefore, writing this book as an ordinary person who was born 21 months after his death, in free India.

As a child I was fortunate to be in contact with people who had either worked with Gandhi themselves or worked with those who were close to Gandhi. Through such people only I could learn a few things about Gandhi from the age of six to the age of twelve. It is obvious that the information my elders gave me was from an adult to a child, still I vividly remember to have developed a feeling in me that enthusiasm towards Gandhi's principles was gradually waning among his followers. They all respected Gandhi but, as I felt, did not have enough faith in the principles of Gandhi.

I was a school going young boy then. Our text books contained chapters on Gandhi. I was enthusiastic enough to participate in all the functions organized on Independence days and Mahatma Gandhi's birthday. I had learned to use spinning wheel and used my skills in such occasions. My teachers appreciated this. However, the only thing our schools taught us was that it was because of Mahatma Gandhi that India became independent. The additional information that my father provided me was that Gandhi was very much concerned about poor and downtrodden.

I, personally, could learn about Gandhi's non-violence through a song of a Hindi film *Jagriti* (Awakening) that had its first line as, "De di hame azadi bina khdga bina dhal, Sabarmati ke sant tune kar diya kamal." [O saint of Sabarmati, it is a wonder that you granted us freedom without using sword or shield.] I became a little confused because I found even the followers of Gandhi, whom I knew, were more appreciative of use of arms by Subhash Chandra Bose than non-violent ways adopted by Gandhi.

Till about 2001 Gandhi occupied very little space in my thoughts and whatever I read about him could not inspire me to think. Science, engineering, some literature, some philosophy, sociology, psychology, Marxism, Socialism, Capitalism, Nationalism . . . I travelled through many paths but Gandhi appeared only very casually in my life. I read a few articles on him. Most of them communicated in a weak voice, 'Gandhi is still relevant'; as if they wanted to say 'Gandhi is not that irrelevant.' Perhaps, modern India considered him a political failure with immature economic principles. Hindus thought that he favoured Muslims and Muslims never talked about him. Hindus of higher caste did not appreciate his idea about revamping Hindu tradition of castes and people of lower castes in whose favour he firmly stood throughout his life did not even remember him. Perhaps Indian society considered him a bit too saintly to strengthen its political and social systems. Religious leaders and spiritual leaders thought him to be a politician involved with mundane issues. However, it seemed India was not prepared to forget him. All big cities of India had their main road named after him as 'Mahatma Gandhi Marg'. All Government offices displayed his nicely framed pictures with a smiling face.

Someone gave me a book on Nathu Ram Godse to read. Godse was the man who assassinated Gandhi. I gathered from the book that during his trial Godse contested his case himself. He admitted his crime but wished to argue for the sake of getting his motive behind the murder recorded. In a nutshell, he argued that Gandhi was pursuing a policy of favouring Muslims and Pakistan; and he (Nathu Ram Godse) being a Hindu citizen of free India wanted him to stop. He argued that Gandhi's stature was too large and that he was so popular in the country that except for Gandhijee's physical elimination he (Godse) had no option to prevent Gandhi from what he was doing. In the court Godse presented some very strong arguments to establish that the Hindus were being made to suffer due to policies of Gandhi. This was for the first time I personally had a glimpse of something inconsistent about Gandhi; at least that was the way I thought about it.

Another important thing happened almost immediately after reading the book on Godse was that I saw the film Gandhi by Richard Attenborough. In this film I could feel Mohan Das Karmchand Gandhi as a man who was struggling to live like a human being. After watching the film I thought I must understand Gandhi.

My own small struggles forced me to delay my plan. It was a blessing in disguise as my struggles made me understand life better. In the year 2001 I read Geeta Bodh (Understanding of Geeta), a book of 95 pages written by Gandhi. It inspired me to read some of the ancient Indian scriptures and some of Gandhi's literature. I saw Gandhi (the film by Richard Attenborough) a few more times.

As such I am a slow reader. Only a few paragraphs push me to deep thinking and imagination about the contents; and reading becomes slow. Literature written by others on Gandhi could not bind me. I left all of them as they all appeared to prove some point or the other and establish what contributions Gandhi had made in which fields. All I can say that I could feel Gandhi by reading what he himself wrote. Gandhi compelled me to introspect. My efforts to understand him helped me to understand many things about myself and also others.

I found Gandhi was much deeper than how he was taken by those who followed him; and many times simpler than how was he taken by those who criticized him.

I decided to share my thoughts with his followers as well as his critics, but more importantly with those who do not know Gandhi.

If my readers are able to gather something useful from my book credit would go to Mahatma Gandhi. If they do not, it shall solely be my failure.

Promod Kumar Sharma

01

GANDHI REVIEWED HIMSELF

At the age of 56 Gandhi completed his autobiography and titled it as *My Experiments with Truth*. He dated the Introduction of his autobiography as 26th November, 1925. Last chapter of his autobiography, referred by him as '*FAREWELL*', has much to say. Let us listen to him.

FAREWELL

The time has come to bring these chapters to a close.

My life from this point onward has been so public that there is hardly anything about it that people do not know.

It is not without a wrench that I have to take leave of the reader. I set a high value on my experiments. I do not know whether I have been able to do justice to them. I can only say that I have spared no pains to give a faithful narrative. To describe truth, as it appeared to me and in the exact manner in which I have arrived at it, has been my ceaseless effort. The exercise has given me ineffable mental peace, because it has been my fond hope that it might bring faith in Truth and Ahimsa to waverers.

My uniform experience has convinced me that there is no other God than Truth. And if every page of these chapters does not proclaim to the reader that the only means for the realization of Truth is Ahimsa, I shall deem all my labour in writing these chapters to have been in vain. And even though my efforts in this behalf may prove fruitless, let the readers know that the vehicle, not the great principle, is at fault.

To see the universal and all pervading Spirit of Truth face to face one must be able to love the meanest of creation as oneself. And the man who aspires after that cannot afford to keep out of any field of life. That is why my devotion to truth has drawn me into the field of politics; and I can say without the slightest hesitation, and yet in all humility, that those who say that religion has nothing to do with politics do not know what religion means.

In bidding farewell to the reader, for the time being at any rate, I ask him to join with me in prayer to the God of Truth that He may grant me the boon of Ahimsa in mind, word and deed.

What have been quoted above are selected portions from the ultimate chapter of Gandhi's autobiography. We shall start our journey from this point. We shall not follow any restrictions about time. We may move to the times prior to1925 or thereafter, as our purpose is to learn about and learn from a life that was lived with utmost honesty.

We select some key expressions from the above. They are;

Truth, God, Ahimsa (non-violence) and 'Love for meanest creation as oneself'.

We shall endeavour to know the meaning Gandhi attached to the selected expressions and try to know if we, after about ninety years, understand them in the same manner as Gandhi did.

I think this exercise is necessary. The purpose of this book is to understand Gandhi. If we are able to know, even partly, what he thought and why he thought what he thought, we will be able to know the intent behind his deeds. Death spares no one. We all leave behind us a few incomplete tasks. Gandhi left many because he initiated many in his lifetime; many more than what others leave.

Many have tried to 'judge' Gandhi on the basis of his deeds and have declared their judgments in his favour or against him. That is exactly I want to refrain myself from. There are two reasons behind this. The first is that I am not at all competent to judge Gandhi. The second is that most of us suffer from the defect of compartmentalizing any life, including our own lives. This defect prevents us from realizing true potential of thoughts and also the intent behind the tasks any one performed or tried to perform. No doubt, I also suffer from this defect. However, for some reasons that I myself, is not very clear about; I strongly desire to contemplate on and comprehend what does the world stands to gain or lose if actions based on Gandhi's thoughts are initiated again or the incomplete ones are allowed to proceed further; and to reach to a logical conclusion.

While I shall be attempting to understand what was behind Gandhi's thoughts, I may be compelled to deal with the philosophical source of Gandhi's thought process. As, such discussions seldom relate to our day to day thinking, we at times; do not find them very interesting. I request my readers to bear with me during some initial pages that are meant to prepare a ground to discuss Gandhi's thoughts.

02

TRUTH

While writing Introduction of his autobiography Gandhi said;

I should clearly not attempt an autobiography. But my purpose being to give an account of various practical applications of these principles, I have given the chapters I propose to write the title of The Story of My Experiments with Truth. These will of course include experiments with non-violence, celibacy and other principles of conduct believed to be distinct from truth. But for me, truth is the sovereign principle, which includes numerous other principles. This truth is not only truthfulness in word, but truthfulness in thought also, and not only the relative truth of our conception, but the Absolute Truth, the Eternal Principle that is God. There are innumerable definitions of God, because His manifestations are innumerable. They overwhelm me with wonder and awe and for a moment stun me. But I worship God as Truth only. I have not yet found Him, but I am seeking after Him. I am prepared to sacrifice the things dearest to me in pursuit of this quest. Even if the sacrifice demanded be my very life, I hope I may be prepared to give it. But as long as I have not realized this Absolute Truth, so long must I hold by the relative truth as I have conceived it. That relative truth must, meanwhile, be my beacon, my shield and buckler . . . . Often in my progress I have had faint glimpses of the Absolute Truth, God, and daily the conviction is growing upon me that He alone is real and all else is unreal. Let those who wish, realize how the conviction has grown upon me; let them share my experiments and share also my conviction if they can. The further conviction has been growing upon me that whatever is possible for me is possible even for a child, and I have sound reasons for saying so. The instruments for the quest of truth are as simple as they are difficult. They may appear quite impossible to an arrogant person, and quite possible to an innocent child. The seeker after truth should be humbler than the dust.

Most religions of the world say realization of God is the ultimate goal of human life. Gandhi accepted it. In fact, the thought of *Moksha* (*Nirvana, emancipation*) was expressed by him from time to time. However, **truth** was his greatest priority. He was uncompromising on the issue of truth. We will see later in this book that ancient Indian scriptures, stories from Indian mythology as well as other religions, particularly Christianity, contributed a great deal in making of Gandhi. However, it was humanity that always compelled him to act in the way he acted throughout his life. This perhaps is the reason why religious/spiritual leaders and other spiritualists never considered him as one of them. They genuinely respected him, at times even very deeply, but he was never called a Saint or considered as a preacher.

Here are a few of his thoughts on truth.

> *Some say God is truth. I say truth is God. I think truth is a word which may be difficult to explain but is very easy to understand.*

> *If one says that he would die for the God, perhaps, neither he nor others would be able to understand what for he was ready to die.*

> *But, if he says, "I will die for the sake of truth." he as well as others will understand what he is prepared to die for.*

(The Diary of Mahadev Desai;
Editor, N.D. Parikh)

Truth hurts sometimes. Saying it politely, that is the best one can do about it, but one cannot always make it pleasing. When you are a seeker of truth you have to call spade a spade. A lie has to be called a lie. There is no option.

(Harijan Sewak; 02.13.1937)

Truth means, what is. Falsehood means, what is not. If falsehood does not exist how can it succeed? If truth always exists how can it be destroyed?

(Satyagraha in South Africa; M.K. Gandhi)

At this juncture it becomes very relevant to pay some attention to what Geeta, a highly appreciated text from ancient Indian scriptures has to say about truth. I quote below 16th Shloka of Chapter II of Shrimad Bagvad-Geeta (popularly referred as Geeta).

"Nasto Vidyate Bhavo, Nabhavo Vidyate Satah, Ubhayorapi Drishtontastvanyostatvadarshibhih."

[Meaning: The first line is simple but very meaningful. It is, "There is no existence of what is not true (Geeta says there is no rule/kingdom of untruth) and there is no dearth of what is true (the truth prevails and pervades everywhere i.e. the rule/kingdom is of truth and truth alone)".

The second line means, "The learned people have concluded that there is only one truth. The truth, the Sat tatva (truth element), is singular."]

Gandhi became acquainted with Geeta because of two Theosophists brothers towards the end of his second year in England. Gandhi has written about this in his autobiography in the chapter, '*Acquaintance with Religion*', Chapter 17 of Part I. Gandhi wrote in this chapter;

I felt ashamed, as I had read the divine poem neither in Sanskrit nor in Gujrati. I was constrained to tell them that I had not read the Geeta, but that I would gladly read it with them . . . I began reading the Geeta with them. The verse in the second chapter

> '*If one*
> *Ponders on objects of the sense, there springs*
> *Attraction; from attraction grows desire,*
> *Desire flames to fierce passion, passion breeds*
> *Recklessness; the memory-all betrayed-*
> *Lets noble purpose go, and saps the mind,*
> *Till purpose, mind and man are all*
> *Undone'.*

made deep impression on my mind, and they still ring in my ears. The book struck me as one of priceless worth. The impression has ever since been growing on me with the result that I regard it today as a book par excellence for the knowledge of truth.

Did Gandhi learn the essence of truth from Geeta for the first time? No, I do not think so. Let me quote some incidents from his autobiography to find the answer to this question.

Childhood (Chapter 2 of Part I)

Mr. Giles, the educational inspector, had come on a visit of inspection. He had set us five words to write as a spelling exercise. One of the words was 'kettle', I had misspelt it. The teacher tried to prompt me with the point of his boot, but I would not be prompted. It was beyond me to see that he wanted me to copy the spelling from my neighbour's slate, for I had thought that the teacher was there to supervise us against copying. The result was that all the boys, except myself, were found to have spelt every word correctly. Only I had been stupid. The teacher tried later to bring this stupidity home to me, but without effect. I never could learn the art of 'copying'.

Yet the incident did not in the least diminish my respect for the teacher. I was . . . but my regard for him remained the same. For, I had learnt to carry out the orders of elders, not to scan their actions.

At the High School (Chapter 5 of Part I)

The reason for my dislike for gymnastics was my keen desire to serve as nurse to my father. (Gandhi's father had met with accidents some time back) . . . Compulsory exercise came directly in the way of this service . . . I

had no watch, and the clouds deceived me. Before I reached the school the boys had all left. The next day Mr. Gimi . . . refused to believe me and ordered me to pay a fine of one or two annas.

I was convicted of lying! That deeply pained me. How was I to prove my innocence? There was no way. I cried in deep anguish. I saw that a man of truth must also be a man of care.

Stealing and Atonement (Chapter 8 of Part I)

But much more serious than this theft was the one I was guilty of a little later. I pilfered the coppers when I was twelve or thirteen, possibly less. The other theft was committed when I was fifteen. In this case I stole a bit of gold from my meat-eating brother's armlet. This brother had run into debt . . . It was done, and the debt cleared. But this became more than I could bear . . . I also made up my mind to confess it to my father. I decided at last to write out a confession . . . I wrote it on a slip of paper and handed it to him myself. In this note not only did I confess my guilt, but asked adequate punishment for it, and closed it with a request to him not to punish himself for my offence. I also pledged myself never to steal in future.

He read it through, and pearl drops trickled down his cheeks, wetting the paper . . .

Those pearl-drops of love cleansed my heart, and washed my sin away . . . Then I could read in it nothing more

than a father's love, but today I know that it was pure
Ahimsa (non-violence). When such Ahimsa becomes all
embracing, it transforms everything it touches. There is
no limit to its power.

My intention behind quoting the above three incidents was
not to say that just because Gandhi as a child possessed the
elements of truth in him he could internalize the thought
of truth from Geeta. My purpose was to show that Gandhi
worked upon himself to firm-up the virtue of truth in his
heart, conduct and speech. He said;

> *Whatever a pure and simple heart feels and*
> *experiences at any moment is truth. Truth*
> *is realized when one sticks to it.*

(Sabarmati Jail, 03.17.1922)

Before we ponder over the meaning of 'Truth is realizes
when one sticks to it', let us try to understand what truth is
for an ordinary human being living in a particular time slot
in the history of this planet.

03

WHAT IS TRUTH?

If we ask anybody about the status of truth in modern times, he would perhaps answer, "Truth is not a very common occurrence in modern times."

Let us agree that whether it is truth or God, we talk about them considering man as the point of reference. Let us begin with an example. When we meet a stranger we begin by having doubts about his intentions irrespective of what he says or shows to us. We are afraid that the other person may 'use' us for fulfilling some of his desires. For instance, if we need an insurance cover, and for buying one we come in contact with some insurance agent, our mind is likely to be occupied with apprehensions that the agent might suggest some policy that helps him earn more; instead of the one that benefits us more.

What may be beneficial for us may not be beneficial for others. Once we stick to this thought, our journey to realize truth starts. There are people whose only interest is to live in luxury to ensure maximum possible satisfaction of their desires. They find ways and means to corner as much resources as possible that are available for use of all. They manage to bring under their control animate resources (animals, fish, birds, plants and, of course men) and inanimate resources (land, water, space, energy etc.)

to satisfy their materialistic desires. Of course, the term they often use for 'their desires' is 'their needs'. In the process of satisfying their 'needs' they often cause harm to those who also have a right to use such resources. History of mankind is replete with instances where some groups of people attacked other groups to acquire control of resources the other groups had under their control. If the attackers could overpower people of groups that were attacked, the defeated ones lost much including their lives and those who survived had to forgo much of what they had or possessed before the attack. In some cultures the defeated ones and generally, also their subsequent generations, had to become slaves of the winners, forever. The conditions of modern world are only a shade different. Some races moved to different lands, used physical force or manipulated situations in their favour with intentions to acquiring control over those lands so that they could use the resources existing there, for their benefit. Those invaders who won became rich and the defeated natives of invaded lands became poor. The rich made great progress in material terms and the poor lagged behind. There is no exaggeration in what has been stated above. Can citizens of a rich country be absolved of the responsibility of causing harm to the citizen of a poor country? Let us not be swayed away with any of the cover-up theories.

Even in one country there are people who are rich because their ancestors deprived many others of what was rightfully due to them (the many others). The future generations of rich have better chances of receiving proper education and developing skills and abilities so as to make use of available opportunities to further enhance their economic and social status. The world is aware that those who are rich are becoming richer and those who are poor are becoming poorer. Statistically, it is said the gap between rich and poor is increasing. It is needless to say that the proportion of people who are wealthy is substantially smaller than those who are poor. That means a small minority of the world is in a position to make use of the very big chunk of worlds resources.

I quote hereunder first two Mantras from Ishopnishad, an ancient Indian scripture, along with their meaning; because these Mantras bring us close to the concepts of 'God is truth' or 'Truth is God'.

MANTRA ONE

Ishavasyam idam sarvam yat kincha jagatyam jagat, Ten tyaktena bhunjitha ma gradhah kasya svid dhanam.

[Translation: All that is animate or inanimate in this universe is owned as well as controlled by the God. One should accept (use) for himself only that much as has been set aside for him (by the God) and should not accept (should not lay hand on) other things, knowing to whom that belong.

Meaning: We all know the laws of nature. Even a small sub atomic particle has a purpose. Existence of one thing depends on another. There is enough for all, even for the smallest of the insects, so that all can happily survive and live their lives. There is no dearth of things that are necessary for one's survival. Mantra says everything in the universe is owned by the God. God owns this nature for the survival of nature itself. Rivers flow to provide water for all living beings, land produces food for all living beings. There is a balance that is maintained so that all that is animate or inanimate can comfortably survive.

Mantra says that one should use only that much as is necessary for his survival and should leave the rest knowing full well that the rest is for the use of others.

If one thinks of having more than what is needed by him there shall be others who will be deprived of what the God has allotted for them (the others). It is a **divine law**. It is the **theory** that has to be accepted as **truth**. If we flout this law by using force, by cheating or duping others, by propounding alternative theories to misguide or misinform others or in any other manner; we will be following what is **untruth.]**

MANTRA TWO

Kurvann eveha karmani jijeevishet shatam samah
Evam tvayi nanyatheto'sti na karma lipyate nare.

[Translation: One may aspire to live for hundreds of years if he continuously goes on working in that way, for that sort of work will not bind him to the law of karma. There is no alternative to this for man.

Meaning: Ancient Indian scriptures say that the actions we do in this life are binding on us and we have to suffer in various life forms (that means we get bound to undergo through the cycles of life and death) if our deeds are not completely selfless and devoted to the divine. That is Law of Karma. The Mantra says that if man follows what has been told in Mantra One he would not bind himself to the Law of Karma thereby improving his chance to enjoy bliss of emancipation, which means eternal happiness forever. The Mantra firmly states that there is no other alternative.]

There is a phrase in Sanskrit which has great relevance in this context. That states;

SATYAM SHIVAM SUNDARAM.

[Satya means truth, Shivam means beneficial and Sundaram implies beautiful. The meaning of the phrase is; what is truth has to be beneficial and what is beneficial has to be beautiful.]

It is not possible for any human being to get rid of sorrow and pain completely although we all aspire for it. Enlightened souls, since time immemorial have been trying to show us the path that leads to eternal happiness. Perhaps many of us are aware of the path, but how many of us have become free from the state of unhappiness?

Unfortunately, much of troubles that humanity is facing are caused by man only. A man may deprive a human being of what is rightfully due to him. A man may make use of a human being; as if he was a commodity; for his convenience and comfort or to satisfy his desires. A man may snatch away fruits of the labour of a human being; forcefully or deceitfully. A man may hurt a human being physically or mentally. All such or similar acts are not consistent with natural laws that exist to sustain and maintain the universe as it should be maintained. Therefore, they are not **the truth**.

'First cause no harm.' That was in essence a part of Hippocratic Corpus, a part of Hippocratic Oath taken by would be medical men, whom we address as doctors. Similarly, a man becomes a human being only if and when he takes such oath.

If a man lives upholding the thought that he would not cause harm to fellow human beings, who undoubtedly, happen to be important components of nature; shouldn't we accept the conduct of such man as **a truthful conduct**?

The thought of causing no harm to anyone or anything that is a part of this universe must be consistent with universal consciousness and that may be accepted as **our relative truth** that we may seek, considering it as our goal.

Gandhi said;

Truth never damages a cause that is just.

(Harijan; 11.10.1946)

Nobody in this world possesses absolute truth. This is God's attribute alone. Relative truth is all we know. Therefore, we can only follow the truth as we see it. Such pursuit of truth cannot lead anyone astray.

(Harijan; 06.02.1946)

I am a humble but very earnest seeker after Truth. And in my search, I take all fellow-seekers in uttermost confidence so that I may know my mistakes and correct them. I confess that I have often erred in my estimates and judgments . . . And inasmuch as in every case I retraced my steps, no permanent harm was done. On the contrary, the fundamental truth of non-violence has been made infinitely more manifest than it ever has been, and the country has in no way been permanently injured.

(Young India; Editor, M.K. Gandhi, 04.21.1927)

My life, so far, has been spent in trying to experiment as to how I can convert what is ideal into what is practical. And I am still continuing with it.

(Harijan Sevak; 02.13.1937)

Gandhi never defined the Relative Truth that he followed (with a desire to reaching close to Absolute Truth) and experimented with. I also could not locate a reliable source to know what he meant by relative truth. However, for some unknown reason, I have developed a faith; (on the basis of his words and deeds I know of) that his relative truth must have been close to what I have written here, that is, under the heading of **"What is truth?"**

04

WHAT IS STICKING TO TRUTH?

In Chapter titled as *Simple Life* in his autobiography Gandhi writes;

> *I once went to an English hair-cutter in Pretoria. He contemptuously refused to cut my hair. I certainly felt hurt, but immediately purchased a pair of clippers and cut my hair before the mirror.*

> *. . . The barber was not at fault in having refused to cut my hair. There was every chance of losing his custom, if he should serve black men. We do not allow our barbers to serve our untouchable brethren. (Here, Gandhi refers to customs of untouchability in caste systems in India.) I got the reward for this in South Africa, not once, but many times, and the conviction that it was the punishment for our own sins saved me from becoming angry.*

**(My Experiments with Truth;
M.K.Gandhi)**

When Gandhi was insulted by an English barber, he must have thought about how painful it is to be insulted by a fellow human being. The feeling of pain made him think about the cause. He found that the pain was caused by a custom that had no respect for humanity which, in turn, made him think about the custom of untouchability and discrimination of the lowly castes in his own country. However, the most important thing was being ashamed of inhuman deeds of one's ancestors. This is what 'sticking to truth is'.

We have already read about the incident given in Chapter 'Stealing and Atonement' (Part I, Chapter 8) of his autobiography. First confession, then asking for appropriate punishment, then committing not to repeat the mistake and finally requesting his father not to punish himself for misdeed . . . that was another example of 'sticking to truth'.

It is not possible to stick to truth without penance. The entire world knows about frequent fasting by Gandhi. The word used for penance in Sansakrit is 'Tapa'. Tapa stands for the process of cleaning through fire just as gold is heated to make it pure unadulterated gold. The seeker of truth has to learn to undergo severest of pain to get rid of what is not true.

Sticking to truth also means 'holding on to truth' or 'insistence for truth'. But if one causes harm to others while insisting on truth, the truth itself may be negated. Gandhi realized the gravity of the problem and continued to dwell into it and carry his experiments with it. He called it "SATYAGRAHA" (Satyagraha means; insistence on truth). He was aware of non-violent resistances that were offered by various sections of the society in past, but his realizations that untruth appears in several forms posed innumerable challenges before him. Gandhi was convinced that truth can be achieved or realized only through non-violent means. Here are a few expressions of his thoughts and feelings.

It is nothing but 'tapasya' (penance) for truth.

(Young India;Editor, M.K.Gandhi))

It is the vindication of truth, not by infliction of suffering on the opponent but on one's own self.

(Speeches, page 501)

. . . often one learns to recognize wrong only through unconscious error. On the other hand if one fails to follow the light from within for fear of public opinion or any other similar reason he would never be able to know right from wrong and in the end loose all sense of distinction between the two . . . . The pathway of Ahimsa . . . one has to tread alone.

(Young India; Editor, M.K. Gandhi)

Rightly or wrongly, I know that I have no resource as Satyagrahi than the assistance of God in every conceivable difficulty and I would like it to be believed that what may appear to be inexplicable actions of mine are really due to inner promptings.

(Harijan; 03.11.1939)

This is high time that I end this chapter on truth. I do it with a burden on my heart that I have miserably failed in my efforts. I feel very small with the thought that what Gandhi could do in most adverse of circumstances that eventually meant a few gun shots taking his life away from him I, on my part, could not explain even an iota of it with all the resources he left for me in form of his writings, speeches and deeds.

Gandhi said, "Truth is God." By the end of the book if I could develop a feeling in me that I am standing at the gate of the truth, I would be satisfied to have made some progress in my life.

05

GOD IS BECAUSE WE ARE

I cannot make you have faith in God. There are things which carry their proofs of existence with them. There are also the things which cannot be proved. There may be cases where heart refuses to accept the God. In other cases, any amount of intellectual argumentation may also fail to develop love and respect for the God.

Keeping all arguments aside I simply say that like crores (tens of millions) *of people I also need God, to lead my life. I am not different from others.*

The starting point is, we are too small to know anything.

(Mahatma Gandhi in England;
Mahadev Desai)

I have found that my knowledge about my work and commitment towards my duties increases when I develop more and more faith in God. I, then, derive more enjoyment from my work. Increased faith

*in God reduces my worries and I become
more patient and careful.*

**(The Diary of Mahadev Desai;
Editor, N.D. Parikh)**

*I have not seen Him, neither have I known
Him. I have made the world's faith in God
my own, and as my faith is ineffaceable,
I regard that faith as amounting to
experience. However, as it may be said
that to describe faith as experience is to
tamper with truth, it may perhaps be more
correct to say that I have no word for
characterizing my belief in God.*

**(My Experiments with Truth;
M.K.Gandhi)**

*I endeavour to see God through service of
humanity, for I know that God is neither in
heaven, nor down below, but in every one.*

**(Young India;
Editor, M.K. Gandhi)**

Hereunder are given two quotations from Pierre Teilhard
de Chardin (1881-1955), a French philosopher and Jesuit
Priest.

You are not a human being in search of a spiritual experience.
You are a spiritual being immersed in a human experience.

Ancient Indian Scriptures reveal that our true nature (*swaroop*) is not in the present form of our existence as human beings, but it is the formless existence of our indestructible Atma (soul). It appears that here Chardin refers to our vertical connectivity with Parmatma (The God) in the above quote. The second quote from Chardin is;

The most satisfactory thing in life is to have been able to give a large part of one's self to others.

This quotation refers to the selfless action (Akarma), Geeta talks about and which Gandhi devoted his entire life for. It is our horizontal connectivity with this world.

While I find a striking similarity in the thoughts of Gandhi and Chardin through the second quote from Chardin, Gandhi did not greatly emphasize on existence of soul (Atma) and its relation with the Almighty (Paramatma). Of course, he never considered such thoughts as pure imaginations. In fact, he spoke about *Moksha* (emancipation) more often than not.

Realization of God, seeking eternal happiness, or making efforts for attaining *Moksha* etc. are matters of individual's realization and conviction and one's responses to his experiences and learning. We cannot and should not raise questions as to why one opts for a particular path and not the other, as long as the final destination remains same. Gandhi was deeply concerned about others' difficulties, pains, and sufferings in a very large framework and thought that one must make every possible effort to reduce such pains and difficulties; hence he chose a particular path.

He had the inclination and ability to respectfully study what others thought about the God and contemplate over it. He did that; and as I believe, gained some very useful knowledge in the process. He must have internalized some of it within himself if that was useful for the task he had taken up upon himself and might have subsequently passed it over to the world after experimenting with it and appending his opinions thereon. His opinions were the outcome of his experiencing and experimenting with the knowledge he gained from various sources. That is why his opinions have substantial practical value. Gandhi was firm and uncompromising on the basic decisions he took but he was not prejudiced about many peripheral aspects of the operative parts of his decisions.

> *Why is there evil in the world is a difficult question to answer. I can only give what I may call a villager's answer. If there is good, there must also be evil, just as where there is light there is also darkness, but it is true only so far as we human mortals are concerned. Before God there is nothing*

good, nothing evil. We poor villagers may talk of His dispensation in human terms, but our language is not God's.

The Vedanta says the world is maya (illusion). Even that explanation is a babbling of imperfect humanity. I, therefore, say that I am not going to bother my head about it. Even if I was allowed to peep into the innermost recesses of God's chamber I should not care to do it; for I should not know what to do there. It is enough for our spiritual growth to know that God is always with the doer of good. That again is a villager's explanation.

(Harijan; 09.07.1935)

All embodied life is in reality an incarnation of God, but it is not usual to consider every living being an incarnation. Future generations pay this homage to one who, in his own generation, has been extraordinarily religious in his conduct. I can see nothing wrong in this procedure; it takes nothing from God's greatness, and there is no violence done to Truth . . . This belief in incarnation is a testimony of man's lofty spiritual ambition. Man is not at peace with himself till he has become like unto

God. The endeavour to reach this state is the supreme, the only ambition worth having. And this is self-realization. And this self-realization is the subject of the Gita, as it is of all scriptures.

(Young India; Editor, M.K. Gandhi)

Belief, therefore, in prophets or incarnations that have lived in remote ages is not an idle superstition, but a satisfaction of an inmost spiritual want.

(Young India; Editor, M.K. Gandhi)

Gandhi was more concerned about the good, that is, maximum good for many. He, perhaps, was more comfortable with that part of God that supported perpetuation of good in the world. He imagined the God to be kind, benevolent, just, strongly supportive of whatever is good and beneficial, powerful, knowing whatever is needed to be known with instant ability to guide man when the man faltered and even taking up things in his hands that man was not able to handle . . . .

A child 'needs' his father. He loves and trusts him unconditionally. When a child is slapped by his father, he (the child) yearns for going back to his father's lap as soon as he can. Even when a child finds and strongly feels that he is slapped by his father due to 'wrong' reasons, he (the child) prefers to remain confused, rather than being critical of his father or start hating or disliking him.

For a child, "Father is a father. Matter ends. He can do anything." The same applies to the relation between man and the God. I do not know whether I am expressing my views or the views of majority of my readers or the views of Gandhi. I have not found Gandhi contradicting it at any point. In fact, when Gandhi says that he needed God like all others who believed in Him; he seemed to universalize the thought.

> *Perhaps, the root cause of perplexity arises from a lack of the real understanding of what God is. God is not a person. He transcends description. He is the Law-maker, the Law and the Executor. No human being can well arrogate these powers to himself.*

(Harijan; 02.24.1946)

How do we explain all the evil that exists, natural disasters, the violence that pervades, 'the eternal pain of human life' . . . when the God is there? Is it a well thought plan of God so that we conduct and act in the right way? Ancient Indian scriptures tell us about *purusharth, the freedom to conduct appropriately in worldly life,* with an objective to reduce sins of earlier births. Gandhi, in the immediately following quotation says, "God transcends description." Are we not restrained or blessed by God with a state of confusion we often enter into while trying to understand Him? Is it not the same state of confusion that the children often have to live with, about their fathers? What divine love and surrender got to do with our intellectual pursuits? Let us not forget that excessive intellectual efforts often blur our understanding. After all, human intellect also has its limitations.

That is why the wise have advised us not to worship another human being as God, even if he has done the greatest of service to humanity. An incarnation of God is loved, respected, disrespected, obeyed, disobeyed and even fought with, when he is in this world; but when he leaves the world he is worshipped like God.

> *In my opinion, Rama, Rahaman, Ahuramazda, God or Krishna are all attempts on the part of man to name that invisible force which is the greatest of all forces. It is inherent in man, imperfect though he maybe, ceaselessly to strive after perfection. In the attempt he falls into reverie. And, just as a child tries to stand, falls down again and again and ultimately learns how to walk, even so man, with all his intelligence, is a mere infant as compared to the infinite and ageless God. This may appear to be an exaggeration but is not. Man can only describe God in his own poor language.*

(Harijan; 08.18.1946)

Perhaps the God is the way one believes him to be. There are billions of people in this world who believe in him. In *Ramcharit Manas*, a very popular poetic creation in praise of Lord Ram, the poet, *Tulsidas* has written, "*Jaki rahee bhavana jaisi, Prabhu moorat dekhi tin taisi . . .*". That means that each one forms a figure of God in his mind according to his own feelings. That is perfectly true. In ancient Indian scriptures several *Rishis* have described God differently. All religions describe God differently. And it would not be an exaggeration if it is said that each one of us has different perception of God. There are many who do not believe in God. For them the God does not exist.

All who have faith in existence of God; believe that God is all powerful and nothing in this world can happen without His consent or will. Gandhi also talked about highly philosophical concepts concerning the God such as quoted below.

> *I talk of God exactly as I believe Him to be . . . I believe God to be creative as well as non-creative. This too is the result of my acceptance of the doctrine of the multiplicity of reality. From the platform of the Jains I prove the non-creative aspect of God, and from that of Ramanuja the creative aspect. As a matter of fact, we are all thinking of the Unthinkable, describing the Indescribable, seeking to know the Unknown, and that is why our speech falters, is inadequate and even*

often contradictory. That is why the Vedas
describe Brahman as 'not this', 'not this'
(Neti-Neti).

(Harijan; 01.21.1926)

But, his faith in God was complete. He has narrated in
Chapter 10 of Part I of his autobiography about how that
faith was formed.

From my sixth or seventh year up to my
sixteenth I was at school, being taught
all sorts of things except religion. The
term 'religion' I am using in its broadest
sense, meaning thereby self-realization
or knowledge of self.

But what I failed to get there I obtained
from my nurse, an old servant of the
family, whose affection for me I still
recall. I have said before that there was in
me a fear of ghosts and spirits. Rambha,
for that was her name, suggested, as a
remedy for this fear, the repetition of
Ramanama. I had more faith in her
than her remedy, and so at a tender age
I began repeating Ramanama to cure
my fear of ghosts and spirits. This was of
course short lived, but the good seed sown
in childhood was not sown in vain. I think
it is due to the seed sown by that good

*woman Rambha that today Ramanama is
an infallible remedy for me.*

[Note: Ramanama means name of Rama. For many
Indians Ram means God himself although technically
Rama is considered as incarnation of God born on this
earth as a King. Here Gandhi is referring to taking God's
name repeatedly.]

*God shows me the path I tread. He is
my doctor also. He never makes any
mistake. He is all powerful. If he wants
some more work to be done by making
use of my fragile body, He would get it
done; irrespective of what these doctors
have to say. I am in the hands of the God.
Please believe me, I am neither afraid of
death nor of living with a body with many
handicaps.*

**(Speech in New Delhi: 01.16.1948 &
Haijan Sevak; 01.25.1948)**

06

WAS GANDHI A DEVOTEE OF GOD?

I think I have the right answer to this question. My answer is that Gandhi was completely devoted to the cause of humanity having total faith in God. I propose to explain the above with the help of following quotations.

I am devoted to none but Truth and I owe no discipline to anybody but Truth.

(Harijan; 05.25.1935)

Some people call me Karmayogi (Yogi whose Yog is selfless action). I do not think I am a yogi of any kind. The only thing is that I cannot live without work. When a good thought is seeded in my mind, I become restless till I am able to convert it into action . . . I take mala (Prayer beads) in my hand to chant God's name only when I am very tired after the day's work and want to sleep. I worship various forms of the God. Some time I worship God in form of my spinning wheel; sometime I worship in from of

Hindu-Muslim unity or sometime in the form of eradication of untouchability. God (Lord Krishna) has said in Geeta, "Those who worship me, I take care of them.(Yog kshem vahami aham.)"

(Gandhi Seva Sangh; Hudli; 04.20.1937)

When I have to choose between two equally good and just alternatives, I toss a coin to decide. You may call it superstition but I believe that then the decision has God's consent.

I think submitting to the God's will is a perfectly scientific method.

(Harijan Sevak; 12.23.1939)

God can be achieved only through love. The love has to be divine not worldly.

(Harijan Sevak; 11.23.1947) & (Speech in New Delhi; 11.16.1947)

I believe that in totality the true nature of human race is to elevate the mankind and not cause his downfall. The unknown law that ensures the elevation of mankind is definitely the Law of Love. The existence of human race and its proliferation amply proves that 'force of life' is much greater than the 'force of destruction'. As for me, I only understand poem of Love.

**(Mahatma Gandhi in England;
Mahadev Desai)**

This modern age of science has many instances when the things that looked to be impossible yesterday have been materialized today. Such scientific successes are no match to successes achieved through spirituality. In short, spirituality is nothing but our 'Jeevan Dharma'(Nature of our life and duties that we have as living beings).

I am aware; it is difficult to explain what successes through spirituality are, without demonstrating them practically. We can understand them through the outcomes of lives of those who have devoted their lives in performing duties that were to be performed by them for having been born as human beings. True benefit of life in this world can never be achieved without making sacrifices. Demonstrating what Jeevan Dharma in true sense is; by itself is of great benefit.

(Harijan Sevak; 09.26.1936)

After having presented what Gandhi said I cannot resist from quoting from New Testament.

Love suffers long, and is kind;
Love envies not; love vaunts not itself,
    is not puffed up.
Doth not behave itself unseemly,
    seeks not her own,
Is not easily provoked, thinks no evil;
Rejoices not in iniquity, but rejoices in the truth;
Love bears all things, believes all things,
    hopes all things,
Endures all things.
Love never fails.

[I Corinthians 13: 4-8]

In part I, Chapter 17 of his autobiography titled as *'Acquaintance with Religion'*, Gandhi said;

> But the New Testament produced a different impression . . . which went straight to my heart. I compared it with Geeta. The verses, 'But I say unto you, resist not evil: but whosoever shall smite thee on thy right cheek, turn to him the other also. And if any man take away thy coat let him have thy cloke too,' delighted me beyond measure and put me in mind of Shamal Bhatt's ' For a bowl of water, give a goodly meal, etc. My young mind tried

> *to unify the teachings of Geeta, the Light*
> *of Asia and the Sermon on the Mount.*

Gandhi said that God can be achieved only through love. We can safely say that God cannot be achieved without love. Of course, the love has to be divine. I have tried to clarify what divine love is with the help of a quotation from New Testament and Gandhi's concept that love cannot be imagined without unconditional readiness to make sacrifices for it and commitment to perform duties that life worthy of human being necessitates. Can we separate our love and concern for the creation of God and our readiness to surrender to the God alone; with a view to finding out, which of the two should be given preference? If one says that the God can be achieved with divine love only, does he mean to say, "Love God excluding Him of His creation." I am afraid; no true devotee of God can dare to say that.

However, an atheist can, perhaps, even with a strong conviction say that he is completely committed to and concerned about all the living beings; and he does not need the concept of God to lead his life. As such, as human beings, do we have any right to force such gentleman to have faith in God?

But, is it at all necessary to carry out a mental exercise of this kind? Firstly, my firm opinion is that it is not necessary. Secondly, I also think that such a question should not be raised. But, I have learned from Geeta and Gandhi that opinions relying completely on human intellect do not show us the path that is fit to be adopted by human beings, who by their nature are prone to make mistakes.

Some say God is an imagination of the weak. Gandhi perhaps would have had no objection. Very humble as he was he always considered him very weak as compared to God.

Gandhi sailed in two boats. He devoted himself to humanity and he also devoted himself to the God. The two boats he sailed on were inseparably and firmly joined with his **shraddha** for the both. What is **shraddha?** That we shall discuss in next chapter.

07

SHRADDHA

We were discussing how Gandhi related himself to the God in last chapter. There we went beyond the limit of discussion and moved to areas of spirituality, religion, Dharma (duty), humanity, love, sacrifice, evil, goodness and several other issues that are not disconnected to mankind. Perhaps the mankind needs God more than the God needs the mankind; hence we discussed many issues that were not directly connected to the God. We must know that both, our intellect and our words, suffer from serious limitations. For example let us pick up a word *'shraddha'* from Sanskrit language. If we think of love, respect, faith, commitment and gratitude all combined into one; meaning of the word **shraddha** emerges but it has a sense of sacredness. We do not say that someone has **shraddha** on devil. What to say about God, at times it becomes difficult to explain even a human being with words and by using intellect. Gandhi said;

> *There are issues that cannot be properly*
> *understood with the help of our intellect.*
> *We have to accept them with shraddha.*
> *Shraddha does not oppose intellect. It is*
> *beyond intellect. We may call it our sixth*
> *sense that helps us in dealing with issues*

that cannot be understood by intellect alone.

(Harijan Sevak; 03.06.1937)

Gandhi also said;

Things that relate to our Atma (soul, spirit) cannot be made to learn or could be understood with the help of intellect. If we try doing it, it would amount to making one have shraddha (in this context faith becomes the most important element of shraddha) *on God with intellectual arguments.*[Intellectual arguments cannot explain God, that is what Gandhi meant here.]

(Harijan Sevak; 06.16.1938)

Faith in God is neither an intellectual issue nor is it an emotional matter. True faith in God falls in the realm of intuition. Those who believe in God know this. Gandhi was no different. Perhaps he was also 'attached' to God in his own way, both intellectually and emotionally, due to his conviction and concern about the pressing needs of humanity. I cannot prove my immediately preceding statement. But, I can try to elaborate. Gandhi said **shraddha** is **beyond** intellect. Our bodies, desires or emotions cannot be beyond intellect. Beyond our intellect we go deeper in the realm which connects to the intelligence that is the cause of everything that exists in the universe. That intelligence is flawless. It creates and takes care of what is created. It is concerned for what it has created. It is not like the concerns you and I have. It is the concern only someone else who is beyond us has. The following shloka in Sanskrit amply and clearly defines His character.

Mookam karoti vaachalam pangum langhayte girim,
Yatkripa tamaham vande Paramanand Madhavam.

[Meaning: He can make the dumb speak with eloquence. He can make the lame cross high and difficult mountains. He is kind, most benevolent, resourceful and powerful. He is the God, always ready to grant us eternal happiness.]

It is our **shraddha** in God that allows our mind to reach to a state of perfect serenity and grants us energy, enthusiasm, self-confidence and faith in accomplishing the most difficult of the tasks. The only condition is that the task must have consent of the God.

At this point, we must understand the true meaning of **faith**. If I say I have faith in God it does not mean that I believe that he exists. It actually means that I am committed to all that He expects from me. The one who has faith in God is not allowed to summon his intelligence to evaluate if what God expects from him is right or prudent; or permit his emotions to find out whether God's expectations would give pleasure to him.

To further elucidate the point regarding faith I refer to an incident from the life of Shri Ramkrishna Paramhans, the teacher of Swami Vivekananda that is self explanatory.

> Someone once asked Ramakrisha if he had blind faith in God. Ramakrishna replied, "Faith is always blind."
>
> *Just as one cannot hear with his eyes, the God cannot be recognized with the help of senses or intellect.*
>
> *You need to have unconditional, unwavering and complete shraddha in God to be able to recognize God.*

(The Diary of Mahadev Desai; Editor, N.D. Parikh)

Not only Gandhi but many others experienced that **shraddha** can do miracles. But, **shraddha** is not something that can be bought at a price or can be learned through books or can be imparted in one through a few training programmes of some fixed durations, conducted by some experts. **Shraddha** is not a tool that can help one achieve some selfish goals or satisfy some selfish desires. God does not expect human beings to use the faculties that He granted to man viz. body, senses, mind and intellect for satisfaction of their ever increasing and insatiable selfish desires or derive pleasures through false sense of pride and dignity; that is to say that personal achievements of man do not contribute to the welfare of God's creation. God is aware that if man starts diverting his abilities and energies in selfish pursuits for deriving momentary pleasures; the balance that exists in His highly complex creation would definitely be disturbed thereby enhancing pain and sorrow in the universe and may cause avoidable damage and destruction.

Therefore, the God lends a portion of his infinite power to only those who commit themselves for the good of universe and have learned to conduct themselves accordingly. In essence, when one develops right thoughts and commits himself totally for the right conduct, he becomes eligible for God's help and support in accomplishing the tasks that God thinks are the right tasks (we can call them 'right actions').

This was the science of **shraddha**. Gandhi might not have used these words but he went about elaborating each and every element of thought and conduct that was essential for obtaining God's grace for selflessly accomplishing the tasks one may take up for the good of the 'whole'; as this was the path of truth according to him.

This book endeavours to discuss some of such elements Gandhi experimented with and subsequently wrote or spoke about.

08

AHIMSA (NON-VIOLENCE)

Non-violence is the universal law which is not limited by time, space and circumstances. It cannot be overlooked.

Neglecting non-violence will amount to self-destruction. The only question which shall then be left, would be, how much time such self-destruction will take.

(Harijan Sewak; 07.15.1939)

Non-violence is the universal law for existence (survival) of humanity. It is operative just like Isaac Newton's law of gravitation. If law of gravitation fails earth shall not be revolving around the sun, moon shall not be circling in its orbit around the earth . . . suns and planets may collide . . . what will exactly happen we don't know. What will happen if universal law of Non-Violence fails?

The entire human society has existed and survived on the strength of non-violence since ages just as the earth is stable in its orbit due to the law of gravitation.

(Harijan Sevak; 02.11.1939)

All the miracles which humanity has witnessed have happened due to silent but powerful actions of unknown forces. Out of such miracles non-violence has been found to be the most silent and with largest impact.

(Harijan Sewak; 03.27.1937)

Gandhi did not invent non-violence. All religions preach non-violence. Ancient Indian scriptures have spoken about it in great detail. No philosopher has written or spoken in favour of killing others. Still, when Gandhi adopted non-violence as a way and philosophy of human life the world looked at him in disbelief.

There is no doubt that human race, in principle, favours non-violence. It favours non-violence because 'it does not hurt' or let us say, it causes no harm.

The world saw Gandhi with his followers, courageously protesting for some just cause peacefully with folded hands, not even using unpleasant words; against forces well equipped with batons and guns, being dragged, beaten badly and pushed into jails and bearing inhuman torture. No one ran away, no one begged for mercy and no one surrendered. All continued protesting to be beaten, dragged . . . even killed.

The good about man is that he is humane. Those who watched sympathized with the protestors.

Fearless and non-violent protestors instilled fear in the minds of violent tormentors. That is how non-violence worked.

Some were impressed with the idea of using non-violence as a tool. Others thought that it could work in a limited way in limited contexts. Some even apprehended that the idea of non-violence would be misused.

In final analysis, all praised Gandhi's non-violence as it was consistent with scriptures and religious messages. No doubt Gandhi's non-violence influenced India. It also influenced the world in many ways. But, could the world understand what was in Gandhi's mind when he adopted non-violence as an extremely important tool?

If India became free of British rule, it was not solely due to Gandhi's non-violent movement. If India was divided into two separate nations at the time of attaining freedom it in no way establishes that the thought of non-violence had failed. If there are wars, terrorism and violence in conduct of people of our times it does not mean that the theory of non-violence as understood and practiced by Gandhi did not have the potential Gandhi thought it had.

Gandhi started his experiments with non-violence in South Africa and continued with them in India till the time of his death. He firmly believed in complete transparency about his deeds and thoughts. He said and wrote about the inferences he could derive through his experiments. The world witnessed those experiments and found much that was encouraging in those experiments. But could Gandhi, in his life time, complete his experiments so as to arrive at some conclusions that could bring about a change in conduct of the people? Could his ideas of non-violence influence socio-political thoughts and actions of next generation leaders?

To make my point clear let me present a very small case of measurement of speed of light. Albert Abraham Michelson (1852-1931) an American Physicist started a revised experiment to measure speed of light late in his life with Francis G. Pease and Fred Pearson but died when only 36 of the 233 proposed observations were made. The experiment was completed four years after his death to give a fairly accurate measure of speed of light to the world. There are tens of thousands of such instances when a single life time was not found to be sufficient to establish a scientific theory. How can we expect that a socio-political theory having the potential to bring about a change in the conduct of the world could be considered as concluded by Gandhi?

The world must know what was the true basis of Gandhi's experiments with non-violence? Praising Gandhi profusely or discarding him thinking his ideas as impractical is not only being unfair to Gandhi but also self defeating.

Truth, non-violence and divine love are central to Gandhi's thoughts and experiments. Out of the three, **non-violence** has great social, political and economic relevance. Is it not important that we explore meticulously, at this stage of human civilization; whether non-violence is the only option we and the future generations are left with? Or, we simply permit Gandhi to exist in the annals of the history as an honest, simple and straightforward politician and social reformer who had a few good ideas worth including in curriculum of humanities and social sciences in the universities world over.

Every year, on or around 2nd October (Gandhi's birthday) I find some space allotted to articles in news magazines that say, 'Gandhi is still relevant today'. I also hear that some of the educational institutions who provide specialized education include 'My Experiments with Truth' in the list of must-read books. But I fail to notice anything Gandhian in our political, economic, social, cultural, educational, administrative or any other systems that matters in my country. If there is anything seriously Gandhian outside India, I am not aware of it.

Gandhi said;

> *It may happen that after me some of you will start turning the pages of Young India or Harijan when you have a problem. A few of you may even try to use them as evidence. If you ask me I will suggest that my writings must be consigned to flames with me. What I have done shall remain. What I have said or written will not remain . . . . If what I have said or wrote has any value then it is only to the extent it has been made use of*

*by you in understanding great principles
of truth and non-violence. If you have not
understood truth and non-violence then my
articles are worthless.*

**(Gandhi Seva Sangh; Hudli &
Harijan Sevak; 05.01.1937)**

History is replete with instances when great thoughts
or works were recognized much later than they were
delivered. If Gandhi never gave up, why should we?

We must continue.

*Non-violence is a conduct. It attains its
full glory when the weak realize their
strength and the powerful realize the
futility of their strengths.*

(Harijan Sevak; 07.26.1935)

Is it not awakening? Five billion people realizing there
strength! Two billion people realizing futility of their
strengths!

*Non-violence should have a capacity
to demolish violence. If this quality of
non-violence is not proved, it should be
considered that something is lacking in it.*

(Harijan Sevak; 05.20.1939)

The statements given above are indicative of the potential non-violence has. Non-violence should never be mistaken as a defense strategy. It is a strategy to bring about a total change for the better; change in the society and change in the individual who acts adhering to the policy of non-violence.

Violence is not confined to use of physical force. Violence can be of mind, speech, conduct, action, thoughts, behavior, attitude etc. The essence is that, what hurts others or cause harm to others is violence. What causes harm to others causes harm to us; hence, what causes harm is violence. One who amasses wealth when others are poor, one who stores food items for months when others are starving, one who sells goods at a higher price when the commodity is in short supply, one who discourages someone who proposes to do good to others, one who makes fun of someone who is handicapped or one who does anything that may hurt/harm others . . . all or each one of them; is committing violence. When a few enjoy fruits of resources that are meant for survival of all; thereby depriving many of what is rightfully due to them; also conduct themselves in a violent manner. It is the duty (Dharma) of the deprived or those who are harmed due to violence of others, to act in a non-violent manner to ensure that the violence as explained above is demolished.

It has become necessary to explain the word Dharma. Often Dharma is used in place of religion, but that is not its correct use. Everything exists according to its 'true nature'. A tree offers fruits to the hungry and shadow to those who are incapacitated due to scorching heat of sun. Therefore, to provide fruits and shadow is Dharma of tree. To provide clean water to many is Dharma of river. To provide knowledge to his students is Dharma of a teacher. In this sense, when we speak about Dharma of man, we use the word duty instead of 'true nature'. To make it more clear let me give a few more examples. It is the Dharma of a father to protect his son and help him grow so that the world is benefitted by his (son's) existence. It is the duty of a ruler to protect and take care of the people over whom he rules. Ancient Indian scriptures have dealt with the issue of Dharma in great details.

It has been said;

"Dharyate iti Dharmah." [Conduct, which must be adopted for the good of all, is Dharma. We know what is good for all actually sustains.]

Scriptures also say;

"Ahimsa Parmodharmah." [The greatest Dharma is non-violence, that is, 'Non-violence is supreme duty of the mankind.']

I find it fit to quote two shlokas of Maharshi Vedavyas, who is believed to have authored some of the precious ancient Indian scriptures and about whom it was said that he was 'Sarvabhootahite ratah' [that may be translated as, 'the one who was always busy for the well being of others'].

> *Shruayatam Dharma sarwaswam shrutva*
> *chapyavadhrayatam,*
> *Aatmanah pratikoolani pareshan na samacharet.*

[Translation: Listen to what Dharma is and what is its essence and after listening to it, conduct accordingly. Do not do any such acts directed to others that you find unbearable for yourself and which cause you pain.]

> *Jeevatum Yah swayam chechhetkatham sonyam*
> *praghatyet,*
> *Yadyadatmani chechhet tatparsyapi chintayet.*

[Translation: One who wants to live, how can he think about killing others? Whatever one wants for himself, he should endeavour to ensure that others also get it.]

Gandhi said;

> *Historical facts that have come to light indicate that man has steadily moved forward on the path of non-violence. Perhaps, in the beginning a man had no problem in killing another man and eating him to satisfy his hunger. Then, they started hating this act and instead of eating each other killed animals to feed themselves. Later, they started tilling land to grow food for them. They started settling down with other fellow human beings in groups taking care of each other.*

Families were formed paving way to formation of societies. Violent tendencies gradually subsided so that mankind can live in peace. Had it not been the history of man, human race would also have become extinct like many other inferior species of animals.

(Harijan Sevak; 08.10.1940)

The thought of non-violence is not confined to abstaining from using physical force. Non-violence is also of mind, speech and deeds (Mansa, Vacha, Karmana). It is applicable to our social, political, economical, national and international lives also.

(Harijan Sevak; 02.11.1939)

Understanding of non-violence can be acquired from one's family itself. If one can succeed at that level only, he can succeed elsewhere also. This I can confidently say from my experience. After all, for one who is non-violent the entire earth is his family.

(Harijan Sevak; 07.20.1940)

Scriptures form ancient India support a concept of **Vasudhaiva Kutumbakam**. [Meaning: The entire earth is a family.] This concept clearly suggests that our benefit depends on the benefit of the earth and we have to be concerned about the entire humanity and our natural environment. By environment our ancestors could have thought of our planet only. Perhaps, they could not have imagined that human beings were capable of causing damage to space also or maybe they had anticipated man polluting even the space because they were well aware of human greed and human intelligence and the disaster a combination of these two could cause.

No doubt, causing harm to our environment is also violence. Basically, at the root of all kinds of violence is mental violence. Gandhi said;

> *Considerable efforts are needed to achieve the state of mental non-violence. Just like a soldier, whether it suits us or it does not, we have to practice non-violence under strict discipline . . . . a high level of this state can be considered to have been achieved when body, mind, intellect and speech all are in perfect unison . . . . For me truth and non-violence are only two sides of a coin.*

(Mahatma Gandhi in England;
Mahadev Desai)

Gandhi considered non-violence as a seed of something like a divine tree to give fruits and shelter to mankind for years and years.

> *The initial steps towards non-violent conduct are adopting and developing qualities of truth, humility, love, compassion, tolerance, patience, benevolence etc . . . . In fact this should not remain as some policy that must be adopted by one, as policies need to be altered some times; they should become principles and laws that cannot be compromised, come what may.*

(Gandhi Seva Sangh, Delang; 03.25.1938) & (Harijan Sevak; 04.09.1938)

Very often Gandhi spoke, discussed and wrote about routine aspects of human behavior as he believed that no knowledge could be considered as acquired unless it is put to practice. Given below is an example of one such discussion on non-violence.

> *It is violent to form casual opinions about others. The followers of non-violence must be extremely careful in this regard. The facts and circumstances about one's birth, growing up, living conditions and compulsions must be thought of before*

finding faults with others. It is the duty of those who have collected around me that they refrain from thinking about others' shortcomings; instead they should think about their strengths. Each one of us should try to win the confidence of others with love, compassion, tolerance and service; crossing the barriers of each other's prejudices.

(Harijan Sevak; 07.27.1940)

Gandhi said;

I value only one thing, which is truth; truth in its totality; even if it cannot be experienced through five senses. It is like Euclidean Line for me. Let it be in the realm of imagination or faith; it exists; hence it has to be explored. The only way to explore truth is Ahimsa (non-violence).

**(Bapu Ke Karavas Ki Kahani;
Dr. Sushila Nayyar)**

To me it appears that for Gandhi life was nothing but a sequential process that he had recognized well, unlike most of us who fail to do so. **It was from non-violence to truth; and then, from truth to the God.**

I have experienced that it is never ever possible to fully comprehend anything intellectually. We either fall short of information and knowledge or we become prejudiced due to our pride for having gained enough knowledge or we suffer from our own intellectual limitations, particularly at critical junctures. We must not forget about limitations of human intellect.

While I am writing this book I am continuously having in mind if I am competent to write a book on Gandhi. This is helping me to some extent in observing my own bias towards or against Gandhi. Although I have not seen Gandhi but I often develop a feeling as if Gandhi is telling me, "Be honest and write what you feel. Do not bother about me."

I did not read Gandhi much or much about Gandhi for a very long period of my life. Out of the little I read, there was also something about the reported arguments his assassin presented before the judge during his trial. Even his assassin, Godse repeatedly spoke, during his arguments, about the respect he had for Gandhi. Strangely, I always found something mysteriously good about Gandhi whenever I was exposed to him through others, irrespective of whatever others conveyed about Gandhi. I had planned this book on the basis of my 'feelings' about him and his thoughts and deeds. Gandhi had the non-violent power of pulling out the good and bringing it on the surface, from all whom he interacted with in person or through his thoughts and deeds.

When I was typing out last few paragraphs, I felt that all of us live, not in disjoint pieces, but in form of some definite process that has its own continuity. This thought is helping me to understand Gandhi beyond my limited ability. My purpose of writing this book had never been to analyze Gandhi in some context or otherwise, as I could not have done justice to that. I am nothing before him that I am very sure of. My purpose was to express Gandhi from the point of view of an Indian born about 21 months after his death, in free India. Whatever I wrote so far was mostly effortless on my part. But from this point onwards I shall try to understand Gandhi keeping in mind the aforesaid sequence i.e. **from non-violence to truth and from truth to the God.** I feel Gandhi carried non-violence from his births that was nurtured by his family. My inner voice says that **non-violence** was at the root of his **truth** later in his life. I submit this thought to my readers with utmost humility.

09

NON-VIOLENCE IS
INTUITIVELY OBVIOUS

We do not have to make truth and non-violence something for use of a few individuals. We have to make them useful for groups, races and nations. At least, I have this dream. I live to realize this dream . . . . Shraddha helps me in this process. Non-violence is in the nature of human soul. It means, all should make use of it (the non-violence) for all the issues concerning their lives.

(Harijan Sevak; 03.16.1940)

As clarified earlier **shraddha** is a feeling that broadly combined respect, faith, love and gratitude and some other qualities. Here, Gandhi means faith and devotion. Soul (Atma) is considered pure according to ancient Indian scriptures. It is said that it is covered with what is not real (what is not truth) due to worldly influences the man gets attracted to, owing to his insatiable desires, frivolous and unsteady nature of human mind, meaningless intellectual activities and the 'I am'-ness (Ahamkara). With knowledge of truth or selfless action or complete devotion to the

Almighty, man can remove the 'covering of the unreal and falsehood' to realize pure soul. That helps man to attain eternal bliss. Such pure soul has no violence. That is why Gandhi said that all human beings can become non-violent, as all of us have souls that can be made to attain its pure state by getting rid of what is not truth. Geeta used the word **"Satva Sanshuddhi"** for the process narrated in immediately preceding discussion.

> *Love and Ahimsa are matchless in their effect. But, in their play there is no fuss, show, noise or placards. They presuppose self-confidence which in its turn presupposes self-purification. Men of stainless character and self-purification will easily inspire confidence and automatically purify the atmosphere around them.*

> **(Young India; Editor, M.K. Gandhi, 09.06.1928)**

> *Identification with everything that lives is impossible without self-purification; without self-purification the observance of the law of Ahimsa must remain an empty dream; God can never be realized by one who is not pure of heart. Self-purification, therefore, must mean purification in all the walks of life. And purification being*

highly infectious, purification of oneself necessarily leads to the purification of one's surroundings.

(My Experiments with Truth; M.K. Gandhi)

But the path of purification is hard and steep. To attain to perfect purity one has to become absolutely passion-free in thought, speech and action; to rise above the opposing currents of love and hatred, attachment and repulsion. I know that I have not in me as yet that triple purity, inspite of constant, ceaseless striving for it. That is why the world's praise fails to move me; indeed it very often stings me. To conquer the subtle passions seems to me to be harder far than the physical conquest of the world by the force of arms.

(My Experiments with Truth; M.K. Gandhi)

Gandhi further said;

Non-violence begins from introspection.

(Harijan Sevak; 04.20.1940)

Whenever we are asked to adopt a new path we become apprehensive of many difficulties. In fact, we have a tendency to resist any change. We magnify trivialities and seek opportunities to abandon the new path, on the flimsiest of grounds, in favour of paths well known to us, that is, the paths we have ever been accustomed to tread. This exactly is the reason why any social change becomes very difficult to implement.

We, as human beings, have become very used to violent conditions all around us. Here, violence should not be taken in the narrow sense of physical violence alone. Extent of violence may differ from one society to another or one set of living conditions to that of another. In one extreme there may be simply unwanted obstructions that irritate us and on the other it could be rape and murder of those who are weak. There may be systems that deprive certain sections of society of resources and opportunities that such sections deserve to get in all fairness. There may be nations that exploit some other nations so that the citizens of exploiting nations could live more comfortably. There may be popular governments in some democracies who actually work in the interests of a few powerful sections of the democracy only because such sections possess the ability to maneuver election processes to ensure installation of governments of their choice. Violence is all pervading. Nuclear families, joint families, groups of individuals, organizations of all kinds, communities, states, nations, group of nations etc, none remains untouched by the influence of violence. There is violence against children, women, old people, physically or mentally challenged individuals, and many others in the human race.

What about us? We suffer due to violence committed by others when we are the target of violence. We, on our part, cause harm to others with our violent acts, words and thoughts, with or without realizing it. It is unfortunate but true that we, in our lives, sooner or later, attain a kind of equilibrium of violence inflicted upon us and violence caused by us. Those who cause more violence than they suffer from; become more arrogant, assertive and shameless; and those who suffer more from violence caused by others than what they are able to cause to others; become timid, miserable and without any self pride or wretched men with deceitful and sly character. I have heard many learned people from within us saying that violence is only a state of mind. Obviously, violence is a state of mind, but is it natural? If that was the case, all violence would have been answered with either violence or by fleeing away to save oneself, just as it happens in the animal kingdom. We all know that human civilizations, good or not so good, have existed in history of mankind; great philosophies and religions were conceptualized in the hope of bringing about changes for betterment of life conditions; and justice had always been a prime thought behind any system intended to control groups of human beings. It means that there had always been something in possession of the mankind that animal never had. The 'hope' for non-violence and peace has always existed, exists today and shall exist in all times to come.

No one knows from where human beings have learned to empower their hopes? They have devised a technique that works more often than not; and that is the technique of developing and having faith.

Voice of soul cannot be expressed through words. Words are physical. Soul is beyond what is physical. Words have limitations. Soul is not limited. Truth can be expressed only through right conduct.

(Harijan Sevak; 12.19.1936)

Our true growth depends on the purity of our soul. Physically, that can be achieved only through building of our character. By having a soul that is pure we become blessed with true knowledge, the divine knowledge.

(My Experiments with Truth; M.K. Gandhi)

Through our honest prayers with total devotion to God we come to know of our true duties. Later carrying out those duties with devotion become our prayers.

(The Diary of Mahadev Desai; Editor, N.D. Parikh)

Gandhi was a man of this world just as we are. He did not subscribe to the hypothesis of the world being some kind of illusion as many spiritualists do. Gandhi believed in spiritual existence of mankind. He believed in God unconditionally as we can see from the quote given below.

Even if a very intelligent person defeats me completely with his strong arguments against existence of the God, I will keep on saying, "Still, the God exists."

(Harijan Sevak; 12.12.1936)

Whenever and whatever he found in this world that was not consistent with God's wishes according to his (Gandhi's) perception he started working on it with a view to setting it right. That was his work and that was his occupation. It seems that he relied on peeping into the territory of The Greatest Unknown, the God, whenever he was stuck. To those, who think I am being illogical, imaginative and very tentative, I beg to submit that most of us also do this kind of a 'peeping in'. Yes, most of us do it whenever we are in great trouble of personal nature. Yes, we pray God, even if we are atheists, when the trouble becomes intolerable and it becomes much beyond our abilities to solve them. Perhaps, pains suffered by others and all kinds of injustice existing in his surroundings quite often placed Gandhi in situations; as we occasionally submit ourselves to when we deeply suffer due to purely personal reasons.

In my opinion, it is neither easy nor difficult for us to appreciate the crisis a lone warrior experiences when violence surrounds him in all forms. Gandhi experienced the violence of all forms that was inflicted upon others; as if that were inflicted upon his own self; he felt a strong urge to resist but finding himself alone, inadequate and incompetent he 'peeped into' the territory of God. He was aware that territory of God was within him with the name of **Atma** (soul). Perhaps, his suffering, his urge to resist, his actions, his feeling about his inadequacy, his 'peeping into' the territory of God through the window of his **soul;** for support and finding solutions and answers to his inadequacy; and finally finding that he is **surviving** despite the onslaught of violence made him develop in himself what he called **shraddha for the cause and faith in success** of his endeavours. Gandhi analyzed that it all began from his **courage** to resist violence. Of course, perhaps, what Gandhi got to learn by simultaneously **being in action** and **'peeping into the God's territory';** was **'how to conduct oneself'** when fighting a battle against violence.

Whether it was "Quit India" movement or his invention of "Satyagraha" in South Africa, whether it was his search for spinning wheel or it was his views on industrialization, whether it was his thoughts and efforts concerning celibacy or atrocities on women; Gandhi never compartmentalized his thoughts. His thoughts emanated from the same source that was an amalgamation of the Truth, the Divine, the concern for the entire humanity, non-violence, love, humility, compassion, courage, care and so on. What he thought, he conducted himself accordingly; and only after acting according to his thoughts he spoke about them.

> *Man becomes what he thinks. But his thoughts are complete only when they are expressed in his conduct.*

> *Conduct regulates one's thoughts. When thoughts and conduct get synchronized the life assumes its true nature (Sva-bhav).*

(Harijan Sevak; 04.07.1946)

10

HUMILITY AND SELF-RESPECT

Humility cannot be acquired through practice. A humble person does not know that he is humble.

Humility means absence of ego (Aham).

If we look at ourselves and the entire universe together, we will become aware of our insignificance. We are not only insignificant but also do not live for long. Humility is the outcome of our realization of our smallness and vastness of the universe. It is an expression of our conviction that we are a part of the universe. Devoting ourselves for the cause of universe or the God is the real meaning and purpose of our lives.

In fact humility means a strong commitment to act. But, that action has to be for the benefit of others, not for fulfilling one's selfish desires.

The God is always busy. He has no time to take even a small rest. If we surrender

to the God we will become a part of him
and then we will also have to act for the
benefit of others. Can a drop of water that
is added to a sea takes rest? It will be in
continuous unrest listening to thunderous
sounds. Those sounds shall actually be the
sound of peace.

(From Yarvada Jail in Madhya
Pradesh; 10.07.1930)

Most of us who have tried to think about life are aware that we human beings are nothing but an insignificant part of universal continuum that is infinite and, perhaps beyond the dimension of time also (at least comprehending its dimensions is beyond us.). Ancient Indian Scriptures suggest that whatever happens in this universe is according to the will of God. Many spiritualists and religions opine that there is nothing absolutely that is in man's hand. Nishkam Karmayog of Geeta inspires one to act, but it also stipulates that fruits of action must be surrendered to the God. The question arises, "What is the right action?" One suggestion that Geeta makes is that an action according to **Dharma** could be the right action. Meaning of Dharma has been explained in the book earlier. In a nutshell it is the duty one has to perform so that the nature with all animate and inanimate included therein, is sustained without being harmed in any manner. Gandhi relied on this. He thought that serving the creation of God is Nishkam Karma (selfless-action).

This thought includes everything that we have discussed so far. Faith in God and surrendering to him; love for God and for all that exists in the world; acting for the benefit of the others, particularly those, who are suppressed, oppressed and exploited by the ones who are powerful, selfish and violent; and causing no harm in the process.

In previous chapters we have seen that non-violence is the tool to achieve the truth. For us, the insignificant parts or components of universal continuum, truth (let us call it 'practical truth' or possibly 'immediately realizable truth' or 'immediate truth'; considering it an step towards absolute truth) could be as small as changing a law that discriminates citizens in using certain compartments of passenger trains according to colour of their skins or as big as installing true democracies in the world (not the pseudo ones) for the people, providing them equal opportunities, rights and responsibilities without any kind of differentiation and discrimination.

We must realize that here, our tool is not some kind of a bolt fastening device but non-violence. We can design an excellent pneumatic bolt fastening device with digital sensors where the only skill that is expected from the operator is to place the bolt and the device in proper locations and pressing a button. In case of using non-violence as a tool, the operator is expected to possess adequate knowledge, temperament, habits, skills, commitment, concern and care to accomplish the task. Further, the operator of non-violence is not working with, say, two blocks of steel gently resting on a work table but he is working on live human beings (fellow human beings, of course) who can resist or respond in infinite ways.

Gandhi was aware of the risks involved in this process.

> *It is more difficult to live for non-violence than to die for it.*

(Harijan Sevak; 01.07.1939)

The risk is not that much of being defeated but of getting involved with violence, irrespective of what kind of violence it could be, whether physical, mental or vocal. For, if that happens, it would mean becoming a part of violence that already pervades to cause miseries in human life.

Humility is a necessary quality that is needed for resisting and eliminating violence from our surroundings. In ordinary language we can say that humility is absence of pride.

One can be proud of his knowledge, wealth, designation, caste or status in society or the material success he has achieved in his life; he can say, "If people respect me it is justified as what I have achieved and acquired I deserved it because of my abilities, efforts and appropriate conduct."

Another kind of pride is being proud of the good qualities one has acquired after making considerable sacrifices. For example one can be proud for adhering to justice irrespective of material losses he had to suffer on this account.

A little thinking would reveal that sense of pride comes from the tendency to discriminate. Discrimination and seeing difference are at the root of violent thoughts and actions. For example, if you have made considerable personal sacrifices for the organization you are working with and on some occasion one of your superior praises another employee (who has made only some insignificant sacrifice in comparison to that of the ones you made) referring to his commitment for the organization; you may feel hurt and your behavior towards that concerned supervisor and that particular employee may undergo a change. It may be appreciated that the seed of violence was sown within you and the root cause was your pride for the sacrifices made by you for the organization.

The essence of humility is absence of pride not only for one's worldly possessions and successes but also for his good qualities and past deeds. Humility is not merely a good etiquette of humbleness, for that could be pretentious also. One can be trained to become humble but one has to work on himself to acquire the quality of humility.

A life of service must be one of humility.
He, who would sacrifice his life for others,
has hardly time to reserve for himself a
place in the sun.

(India of My Dream; M.K. Gandhi)

Gandhi has gone to the extent of saying that even a simple inappropriate conduct of an operator may push him away from his path.

Truth without humility also suffers.

> *Truth without humility will be an arrogant caricature.*

(Truth is God; Editor, R.K.Prabhu)

I will request my readers to recall the first chapter of this book wherein I have quoted the following portion from *My Experiments with Truth*, Gandhi's autobiography;

> *To see the universal and all pervading Spirit of Truth face to face one must be able to love the meanest of creation as oneself.*

Gandhi was referring to genuine humility thereby. 'Believe that you are a cipher' that is what Gandhi suggested. But he also wanted his followers to have faith that they can become men of extraordinary calibre when they have **shraddha** in their work and in God.

There is also a need to differentiate between Pride and Self-respect. Gandhi said;

> *Pride is shallow. Self-respect is deep.*

Self-respect cannot be hurt from outside. As against this, pride always gets hurt from outside (by others or due to external causes).

(The Diary of Mahadev Desai; Editor, N.D.Parikh)

There is also a subtle difference between self-respect and pride. True self-respect can elevate us and pride often causes our downfall. A self-respecting man feels ashamed of his misconduct or bad conduct. If he immediately acts to rectify the errors committed by him and ensures that such errors are not repeated in future, he uplifts himself.

Gandhi said;

Man is a puppet of his follies. When he realizes his mistakes and rectifies them he moves forward; but, if he hides them he becomes animal. Man is neither God nor an animal. Repentance and self-purification (satvasanshuddhi) help him to get rid of his mistakes and shortcomings; and also to wash away his sins.

(Harijan Sevak; 04.21.46)

To err is human. Similarly, to rectify the errors committed is also human. Not making error is the nature of God . . . .

*Making mistakes and not rectifying them
is devilish (Asuri) nature.*

(Harijan Sevak; 01.23.1037)

Geeta has used the word *Hreemh* for shame. Being ashamed of acts, deeds and thoughts that are not according to the will of the God or are not consistent with the duties towards humanity (*manav-dharma*) is a quality that is liked by God. A self respecting individual possesses this quality.

For Gandhi service of humanity was his 'immediate truth' or 'practical truth' that he wanted to realize. He picked up non-violence as a tool to realize this truth. Serving humanity meant reducing the miseries of many. Man can do only that much which is humanly possible. Man himself had been responsible for causing pain to man in most cases. Violence was identified as the enemy number one. How does one resist violence? Rishis, saints, the learned and the wise; all were for non-violence. People listened to them, liked them, respected them and helped them in spreading their messages. The rulers and the powerful were not deaf for their messages of peace but they ruled with swords in their hands. It has been happening since time immemorial; it was happening in Gandhi's time and is still happening.

Gnadhi thought differently. He said, "Violence must end." That meant violence should not be considered as a tool to combat violence. In his opinion non-violence was not an option; it was a compulsion.

I do not think Gandhi took much time in deciding his course of action because he took it intuitively. Intuitions do not appear from thin air. Their source is divine intelligence riding on human intelligence.

I dare to give expression to Gandhi's *intense resolve;*

> To move forward on the path of truth and service to humanity; to resist whatever comes in the way; and to resist with an objective to demolish it completely; but resist it non-violently.

Then, his work started. How to make non-violence win? In Sanskrit language we can use the word **Sadhan** for tool. Learning and practicing how to use the tool (**sadhan**) is called **Sadhana.** One who **voluntarily decides** to become an operator for the proposed tool and is committed to learn the science, art and technique for using the said tool is called **Sadhak** in Sanskrit.

One cannot force, tempt or misguide someone to become **non-violent warrior.** As against this there could be many ways to deploy violent warriors because violence does not need man with quality and character to defend it. Violence is devilish. It is shameless. It has no self respect.

A true Sadhak cannot be tempted, forced or misguided to become a violent warrior. Gandhi invested most part of his life in thinking, experimenting and experiencing as to how to build an army of **true sadhaks.**

Gandhi said;

> *People may call me Mahatma but I never imagined even in my dreams that I alone have the strength to shake India from her existing position. If people listen to what I have to say; think about it and internalize it; and make it known to others also; then we may consider that the task before us is likely to be accomplished. Please do not complain that this man talks to only a few and wants all to do his work. I want to reach to crores, but that is possible if I try to reach to a few with my message with a request to circulate it further.*

(Harijan Sevak; 02.26.1938)

11

COURAGE

Lesson of non-violence cannot be taught to those who fear death and do not have courage to face adversities . . . . The first lesson on non-violence commences from developing courage to stand erect with chest open before an opponent of the size of a mountain.

(Harijan Sevak; 07.26.1935)

Absence of fear is courage. What causes fear? Apprehending loss of something that we are attached to causes fear. We are attached to our bodies. When we apprehend that damage may be caused to our bodies we become afraid. When we apprehend that someone or something dear to us may no longer be with us, fear grips us. There may be fear of loss of money, wealth, source of income, comforts that we are accustomed of, our reputation, our social status etc.

Fear is natural. We have been granted this emotion to protect us. All living beings are instinctively fearful to some extent or more. What is the problem with fear then? Let us take a case that many of us have experienced. Imagine we are travelling in a car driven by someone else and we see a barrier ahead to stop bigger vehicles. The one who is driving knows very well that the car can pass through the barrier and continues driving without slowing down, but we duck when the car approaches the barrier unmindful of the fact that there is a roof over us.

If we travel quite often on the same road that has the barrier referred in last paragraph we would not behave in an instinctive manner. We would have known that our fear was unfounded. Does it not apply to most of our fears? Even a pet dog learns what it should not be afraid of. We are human beings, an advanced species with intelligence many times superior to the most intelligent animal. All of us will die when our time comes. What we possess today might not have been with us earlier and may not be with us in future. Are we not aware of these facts?

We are human beings and are capable of getting rid of our miseries to a great extent. We all know this. Our history provides enough evidence for how much we have come forward. There are things that make our lives miserable, every day, every hour; but we do not make effort to change our plight? Why? Is it not simply because of our fear that we might lose what we have today? We suffer, because we are afraid of suffering. Is it a rational behavior?

Are we human beings that are afraid of other human beings? We are fearful of those human beings that have intimidated us to deprive us of what was rightfully due to us. They intimidated us because we could be intimidated. We were cowards. We were not courageous enough. They intimidated us because they knew that we lack courage. The cheated us because they knew that we could be maneuvered easily. They tempted us because they knew that we would not be able to resist temptation. They took advantage of all our weaknesses and placed us in a state where life became a synonym of misery.

This was the long and short of how some human beings caused harm to many human beings. The first and foremost requirement to come out of that miserable state is getting rid of our weaknesses.

> *Non-violence is the quality of man of strength. Weakness and non-violence cannot walk hand-in-hand.*

> **(Harijan Sevak; 11.04.39)**

> *A nation loses its freedom because of its own weakness. The moment it gets rid of its own weakness it regains its freedom. No race on this earth can be made a slave without helping, willingly or unwillingly, those who intend to enslave it.*

> **(Mahatma Gandhi in England; Mahadev Desai)**

> *Just as one has to learn how to kill while being trained for violent action, one has to learn how to die when being trained for*

non-violent action. There is no freedom from fear in violence but there is enough scope for finding ways and means for avoiding incidence of fear. In non-violence there is no place for fear. The Sadhak of non-violence has to develop in himself the quality of sacrifice. This quality has to be of the highest order. He should not bother about any loss; whether it is land or wealth or even one's life. Who has not won over all types of fear cannot observe non-violence in its totality.

Sadhak of non-violence can have or rather should have fear of God and no other fear. One who is devoted to God must know that soul (Atma) is different from body. One, who knows that soul is indestructible and imperishable, looses all attachment with the body that is destructible by its nature.

The training for non-violence is opposite to that of the violence. For protecting whatever is external one may need violence sometimes but for protecting one's soul and self respect non-violence is essential.

(Harijan Sevak; 08.31.1940)

Risk

In violence risk is an option but in non-violence it is a compulsion. Those who adopt the path of violence sometimes decide to take risk to get into a position of greater advantage. For example, a commander may decide to take a risk of capturing a very well protected post of the enemy to gain a strategic advantage over his enemy in an impending war. Similarly, a smuggler may take a risk by overlooking a possible trap if there is a possibility of making a huge gain. In both of the cases given above there were options of not taking risk.

In, non-violence, the Sadhak has virtually no option. If there is an opprtunity of demolishing some violence it must be availed of. Sadhak knows that if he intends to wage a non-violent war, its purpose is to provide relief to those who suffer in the hands of violence. He knows each win matters to him. In most cases it is the extreme suffering of have-nots that compel them to protest and resist. Those who suffer know it well that they cannot match the violence of their tormentors. The Sadhak who is committed to 'fight' for them and with them knows that violence is not an answer to violence. They have no option. If they win, it is fine but if they die; they would become examples for those who are suffering due to violence.

The one who has adopted the path of non-violence tests himself by taking risks. In short, the courage of one who is non-violent is much superior to that of the one who is violent.

(Harijan Sevak; 08.31.1940)

Non-violence is a weapon of the strong, not of the weak. Strength has to be that of the mind and heart. Physical strength has little meaning. In a war killing or getting killed is common; but bearing violent attacks without retaliation is the courage of much superior form.

(Mahatma Gandhi in England; Mahadev Desai)

At the core of any non-violent conduct, there always exists a strong faith that whatever man does is inspired by the God. This faith does not appear unless and until one has shraddha for the cause.

(Harijan Sevak; 07.19.1942)

I can easily imagine a fearful person all decked up with sophisticated arms. Keeping arms may not be associated with cowardice always, but one can find a ghost of fear hidden somewhere behind the arms. True courage is not possible without true non-violence.

(Harijan Sevak, 07.15.1939)

Fear always injures the fearful. How a fearful person reacts to the people who cause fear? He can run away, can beg for mercy, can attempt to dupe or misguide the offender, can try to weaken the offender remaining in the state of fear himself or he can try to weaken the offender after making himself free from all fears. If any of the first four alternatives are selected the oppressed person (the one who is fearful) would be defending himself from an inferior position to that of the oppressor. Moreover, even if any favourable results are obtained that may be temporary thereby leaving enough scope for re-emergence of offences. When the fearless person shuns all fears he becomes superior to the offender in many respects. But, when he adopts the path of non-violence after freeing himself from all fears he becomes superior to the offender in all respects. He can even gather an ability to make the offender free from all fears and violence.

The oppressed must first free themselves from all fears. Non-violence comes second.

> *Evil is no remedy for evil. When evil is answered with evil, it is not removed; instead it enhances and becomes more powerful. Any violence cannot be eliminated by making use of bigger and more powerful violence. This is a natural law.*

> *Sometimes it may seem that violence cannot be fought with non-violence. But, it should not be misconstrued to mean that the one who is non-violent should surrender to the one who is violent.*

One who is non-violent should never surrender to any unjustified demands and evil designs of those who are violent. Do not surrender to what is not justified till death; that is the essence of saying that violence should not be faced with violence.

(Harijan Sevak; 03.30.1947)

Without having any hard feeling or enmity towards any one and sticking to the knowledge that true existence is of our souls, not bodies; firmly refusing to bend before any violent power, howsoever great it may be; is true act of bravery.

(Harijan Sevak; 10.15.1938)

Violence is falsehood. It is not truth. Truth must be upheld. There cannot be any argument on this point. Not submitting to what is not consistent with humanity is an 'immediate truth' for us, who are human beings. This truth also must be upheld. There are two truths. The former is close to the absolute and the latter is the practical truth (immediate truth) that we need to reduce the pains caused by human beings to human beings.

Do we have an alternative but to resist violence? Some are strongly opposed to violence. They do not favour any kind of violence. They say do not resist because even offering a resistance is violence. They also propagate it through their preaching. Gandhi has the following to say about them;

> *There was non-violence in past also. But, that was a personal affair of a few. Such non-violent persons fled away to hills or preferred to live in some secluded places in villages. They did not take interest in public life and in the affairs of common people. I have started a new tradition.*
>
> *The non-violence that is confined to individuals only is not a Great Duty (Param Dharma) for the mankind. If someone is following non-violence lying in his cave, I shall not worship him. His non-violence is of no use to me. I am in favour of that non-violence that can be used for this world and the humanity. If one achieves Nirvana (Moksha, emancipation) strictly following the path of non-violence but abandoning the world and the people who live there; I do not need such Moksha. I do not need Moksha where I alone am emancipated and others remain deprived of it.*

I will prefer emancipation through continued selfless service.

(Gandhi Seva Sangh; Delang, 03.26.1938)

It was not only a thing of past, even today there exist spiritual leaders in huge numbers who keep themselves absolutely disconnected with public life and politics, under the pretext that they do not want to get involved with illusionary aspects of life. They preach that one should endeavour to purify himself and aim for surrendering to the Almighty as that is the real purpose of life. Even politician do not encourage the spiritual leaders to interfere in the matters of public life. Religions have become sects who give great importance to ritualistic aspects of religions and thereby insist on maintaining a separate identity of their own. Dharma, the duty one has towards the humanity, is being considered as synonym of religion with ritualistic and separatist connotations. A great majority of spiritual leaders, with a view to popularizing themselves for pecuniary benefits are busy in justifying materialistic success as a natural and sometimes even important ingredient of spiritual growth. All of them have little or no concern for pervading violence that is becoming a serious cause of suffering of a very great majority of humanity.

Today violence virtually and commonly is taken as to mean only physical violence. Peace means absence of war. And God means a power whose only job is to give; without demanding anything in return from the man.

Gandhi's concept of "From non-violence to truth to God" has vanished due to technological storm that thunders to say, "How to do is more important than what to do."

Are we learning the art of turning our heads away from violence that prevails in this world? Gandhi said;

> *One who starts trembling or runs away when he sees two people fighting is not non-violent. He is a coward.*

(Sevagram; 08.25.1940)

Whatever non-violence we have today is of the timid, the unconcerned and of those who have dubious intentions. Violence thrives in such conditions. Are we about to enter into the age of systematic violence? Or we are already there?

12

FORGIVENESS

Heaven and earth both are within us. We are somewhat aware of the earth but we are totally unaware of the heaven within us.

(Harijan Sevak; 09.26.1936)

Till the time, when even a single good person exists in this world, I would say this world belongs to good people. If the last good person ceases to exist in this world, the world would, then belong to the devil . . . In fact evil is the devil. If we deeply contemplate, we will find that thoughts, efforts and penance of one good person are enough to carry this world.

(Harijan Sevak; 05.04.1947)

Only the one, who has authority and strength to punish, can forgive. Causing harm to others intentionally is crime. The one who commits crime is called criminal. If one who has authority and strength to punish a criminal, does not punish him even after full knowledge of the crime is considered as having forgiven the criminal. However, his act of forgiveness will be true forgiveness only if the person who forgives is free from any fear or self interest in doing so. A father forgives his grown up son who has committed a crime because he is attached to his son. We forgive a powerful person who has stolen our money because we are afraid that he would retaliate. Women, who are teased or molested by ruffians in busy streets, forgive the offenders as they are fearful of the ruffians as well as of the society that has scant concern and respect for the dignity of women. Police, often avoid registering a criminal case against ministers and other influential persons. Such instances cannot be considered as those of forgiveness.

Gandhi said;

> *Forgiveness is the quality of the soul and therefore is a positive quality.*

(The Mind of Mahatma Gandhi; Prabhu & Rao)

A lot has been spoken in favour of this quality. The concept that is accepted by many great philosophers is, 'God forgives us, and therefore we should forgive others.' The beauty of this concept lies in the fact that if one forgives considering it as his pious duty it does not generate pride in the forgiver.

Forgiveness elevates one spiritually. This part is accepted; but how does it help the one who is forgiven? Gandhi did not want Moksha for himself if that was granted to him alone.

If we have some good qualities like that of benevolence, compassion, gratitude, being truthful in our conduct and say, forgiveness also; then let us ask ourselves how we acquired these qualities. There are very bright chances of our finding out that we had been at the receiving end of these qualities sometime in our past. We give what we get; this rule applies very often in our lives.

When we forgive someone selflessly, without any compulsion and with humility, there are fair chances that someone is prevented from abandoning his goodness.

Gandhi said;

> *Goodness begets goodness. Love begets love. Instead of taking revenge it is better to leave the evil doer at the mercy of God; except this I do not know any other way.*

(Harijan Sevak; 10.05.1947)

It will appear very good if I continue to argue in favour of forgiveness but I am confident that many would doubt if it could really be adopted in totality in our society to produce the results one would happily accept.

The question is whether we are more concerned about the good that exists or the evil that exists. In his autobiography

Gandhi gave several instances when he was ill treated by someone or the other, especially in South Africa. While doing so he also gave accounts of few others who did not mean any harm to him. For example, in the chapter titled as *'More Hardships'* in Part II, in his autobiography when despite Gandhi having a I Class ticket he was told by the guard to shift to the third class from the first class compartment he was travelling in; an English man supported Gandhi. Gandhi never thought ill of anybody who offended him. His conduct never showed that he might retaliate. He simply insisted for what was just. This precisely was the reason that he, almost always, gained support even from the opposite camp. In his conduct Gandhi was a 'compulsive forgiver'. He, courageously, persistently and often irritatingly agitated against the issues that were not justified according to his conscience but invariably 'forgave' those who were backing the issues Gandhi protested against.

Gandhi always viewed the evil and the one who was responsible for causing the evil, as two separate entities. He directed all the violence that he might have had against the evil and spared the 'evil doer' completely. He said;

> *Whatever is inside us is always reflected outside. If you are good world shall be good with you. As against this if you permit a desire within you to consider someone as bad; there is a likelihood that the bad is within you.*

(Harijan Sevak; 05.05.1946)

While one should be very strict in examining himself, he should be lenient in examining others. This is the right policy.

Experience tells us that howsoever strict we try to become in examining ourselves, in the end we tend to become lenient. We always judge ourselves with kindness.

About others, we hardly know enough . . . . Even when we try to be lenient toward others, there are chances of our becoming critical and restless with them. This is the exact reason why we are never able to take as much work from others which they are capable of delivering.

When we are kind and more lenient toward others chances of success that lasts, increase.

(Harijan Sewak; 02.20.1937)

Man is not bad by nature. This has been repeatedly experienced by many. We should never get disheartened about the nature of human beings.

(Harijan Sewak; 11.12.1938)

We have seen that true forgiveness absolves the forgiver of avoidable violence and reaffirms the faith in mankind that human beings are never inherently evil by nature. Not practicing forgiveness is often counterproductive. A society that does not give due importance to forgiveness considers that its job is over after punishing the criminal. In modern times when people become aware of a serious crime having been committed, the leaders, the people and the media unanimously decide, "Book the criminal and punish him hard". Once this is done all have a sigh of relief thinking that the job has been accomplished. In all such situations, the crime is sent to background and the entire attention is diverted to the criminal. In this process the crime is rarely harmed. At best we are successful in sending the crime in hiding for a short while. It resurfaces again. A little thinking would reveal that often only a few violent minds that committed the crime invoke violence in many minds due to faulty concept that at the root of the crime there were a few human beings.

A genuine forgiver is one who with courage and conviction targets the crime and acts to eradicate the evil. Eradication of evil is not an easy job. It is a long drawn battle. It is the job for a brave not cowardly. Gandhi said;

> *Forgiveness is the quality of brave, not of the cowardly.*

(The Mind of Mahatma Gandhi;
Prabhu & Rao)

13

PENANCE

— ·⚬✦⚬· —

Bearing all kinds of hardships for the right purpose truthfully softens the hardest stone. Penance is unique in its effectiveness. This is the key for insistence of truth.

(Satyagraha in South Africa;
M.K. Gandhi)

The one born as a living being has to bear with hunger; pains of body and mind; troubles caused by nature; and what is generally known as acts of God. Ancient Indian scriptures classify the pains that one has to bear as Adhyatmik (related to the self), Adhidaivik (acts of God) and Adhibhautik (related to other physical things that include animals etc.). As one has to bear with all these troubles, more or less, one must bear with them considering them as natural consequences of having been born. Human beings are superior species. They have to find meaning and purpose of their lives. If the purpose has been identified as serving selflessly creation of the God (that is what lower species also do without knowing it) then one has certain duties to perform in his life. While performing those duties some or many troubles would definitely arise. Bearing all hardships and pains that come in our way during performance of our duties truthfully is penance. Penance elevates us.

The operators (**sadhak**) of tool (**sadhan**) of non-violence need to be more committed, concerned and careful about his penance. The **sadhak** cannot ask, 'How much?' or 'How long?' He would not even be able to know in advance what kind of pain he would be required to bear.

Gandhi said;

> *The suffering does not know itself and never calculates.*

> **(The Mind of Mahatma Gandhi;**
> **Prabhu & Rao)**

If we contemplate a little deeply we will realize that experiencing is learning. Many books, many lectures and many written texts cannot provide the knowledge that can be gained by experiencing and experimenting. Suffering is an important skill that can bring peace. Following quotation of Gandhi explains this phenomenon and penetrates deeper to dig out clearer understanding on how suffering can be used to bring about a positive change.

> *Things of much importance for the people cannot be gathered by simply appealing to the intellect of others and by convincing them with flawless logical arguments. They have to be bought at the cost of rigorous penance.*

Suffering is the law for human beings and armed battle is the law of the jungle. Suffering works on the conscience of our opponent who relies on violence and hence not accustomed to paying heed to non-violent appeals. Suffering has infinite power to make him hear the voice of reason. I have prayed in utter disappointment so many times that I cannot recall. Those prayers have helped me to arrive at a firm conclusion that one can make his point understood by his opponent by knocking at his heart and not at his intellect alone. Intellectual appeal touches the intellect alone. For making a way to his heart, how much hardships one has tolerated and how much pain he has suffered; counts. Suffering helps one to enter into the conscience of the other. The legacy humanity carries is of suffering and not of the sword.

**(Mahatma Gandhi in England;
Mahadev Desai)**

Reason has to be strengthened by suffering; and suffering opens the eyes of understanding.

(Mahatma; D. G. Tendulkar)

*My method is conversion, not coercion;
it is self-suffering, not the suffering of the
tyrant.*

(Mahatma; D. G. Tendulkar)

*Love can never express itself by imposing
suffering on others. It can only express
itself by self-suffering, by self-purification.*

(Mahatma; D. G. Tendulkar)

Gandhi invariably preferred to use Sanskrit word '**Tap**' (
Tapasya) for 'penance' or 'suffering'. Here, it becomes
important to clearly understand what Gandhi intended
to express when he used these words. There is no doubt
that Gandhi heavily relied on the purport of Geeta while
expressing his thoughts. It shall be more appropriate to
say that his thoughts arise from what he found in daily
life after contemplating on the intent and content of
Geeta. He interpreted Geeta in his own way and that he
briefly described in his book, Geeta Bodh (Understanding
of Geeta). His understanding of Geeta helped him to
understand all that was happening around him. Often, he
bravely and without being bound by the conventions of
the society, applied the theory he had learned from Geeta
and other sources (he revealed the source along with
whatever he understood from such source) practically
on all the situations, happenings and on his own actions.
He then watched carefully the outcome of his actions
and/or the effect of such applications. He was mostly

uncompromising in his efforts. His views and ideas were basically the outcome of his 'experiments'; that is applying a theory (as understood by him) on his own actions and the external occurrences.

Many have deeply contemplated on the intent and content of scriptures to extract the truth to gain knowledge. Gandhi experimented with the intent and content of scriptures, under strict discipline, to gain practical knowledge with the sole purpose of reducing sufferings of mankind inflicted upon by the mankind.

Scientific laws are made on two considerations; theoretical and experimental. Sometimes theories are evolved first and confirmed experimentally later. Alternatively, theories have to be evolved for making sure of what was experimentally found. Gandhi dared to do both. And he dared to do it, knowing full well that in his case the experiments themselves had the capability of influencing the experimenter.

Notwithstanding the above, I think it would be dishonest on my part if I do not refer about some doubts I have about his being always very impartial and objective in his experiments. Gandhi himself was very disciplined and strict in all matters related to him. He was fearless and absolutely selfless.

The only thing he perhaps did not like was being considered partial to anybody. I am too small to comment on someone like Gandhi. Therefore, I will prefer to repeat what I just said lest my comment is taken in a manner that is different from what I intend to say.

Gandhi was not partial towards himself or his family or any particular person. But, he was fearful of the idea of him being called partial towards any individual or group of individuals.

I am aware that my doubt cannot be resolved intellectually. Apart from accepting my intellectual limitations I have to say that a man can never be a God and dividing line between Dharma (duty) and Adharma (what is contrary to duty) becomes so thin sometimes that nothing can be claimed to be right unless God intervenes.

I apologize to my readers for such interludes as the one above. I am helpless. I am trying my level best to be honest.

To serve humanity selflessly was the meaning and purpose of life of Gandhi. He had nothing else in his mind. He sought peace for himself by waging a war against pains inflicted by human beings on human beings. This war was unimaginably excruciating because it was a war fought between non-violence and violence. Gandhi devoted the outcome of the war that is the fruit of the war to the God and kept for him the fruit of penance the war could not have been fought without. That is why I think it was necessary to quote Geeta here because Gandhi had deep **shraddha** for Geeta. Gandhi said;

I feel very happy to say that I have same respect for Bible, Quran . . . and other scriptures that I have studied, as that I have for Geeta. Study of scriptures of other religions has further enhanced my shraddha (respect) for Geeta.

(The Diary of Mahadev Desai; Editor, N.D. Parikh)

Given below are **shlokas from 14 to 19 of Chapter XVII of Geeta.** The meaning of shlokas is given under each shloka in a manner so that one can read the meaning in English without having to read shlokas in Sanskrit. Those who are interested in shlokas given in Sanskrit may read them.

Devadvijagurupragyapoojanam shaucham aarjaavam, Brahmcharyam ahimsa cha shariram tapa uchyate.

Worshipping God, deities, Brahmins (who have studied scriptures and have gained knowledge there from, the learned and/or those who have made themselves free from the worldly aspects of life; observing complete cleanliness of body and thoughts; possessing utmost simplicity in living, in thinking, in conducting themselves and in speaking; observing celibacy of body and thoughts; and sticking to non-violence, whether physical or that of mind; is classified as penance of the body. In short devotion to truth, cleanliness, simplicity, celibacy and non-violence of body and mind are called **bodily penance.**

**Anudwega karam vakyam satyam priyahitam cha yat,
Swadhyaya abhyasanam cha aiva vangmayam tapa
uchyate.**

Speaking in a manner that does not agitate the minds of the speakers and the listeners; that contains only truth; that does not hurt or harm the listener in any way and has the intent to benefit and please the listener; observing practices that help in gaining true knowledge and having strong will to do so; is classified as **vocal penance.**

**Manah prasadah saumyatwam maunam
atmavinigraha,
Bhavasanshuddhih iti aitat tapah manasam uchyate.**

Happiness of mind, gentleness, practicing silence, full control over mind and purity of thoughts are the characteristics of **mental penance.**

Mental penance needs considerable elaboration because if the words used above are taken in literal sense only the purpose will not be served.

As such happiness of mind depends on space, time and circumstances but there are some crucial factors that provide true happiness of mind. Happiness that does not last long may simply be termed as a particular emotional state. Factors that provide happiness of permanent nature are; absence of attachment or hatred towards people, objects, happenings, states and situations; not being partial towards some on selfish consideration; absence of false pride caused by materialistic possessions or one's good qualities; possessing the qualities of compassion, benevolence, forgiveness etc.; concern for living beings; quality of not being excited if there is a gain and not being dejected when there is a loss etc. These are only some of the important factors that can help in remaining in a state of happiness that is not short lived.

Similarly, gentleness is not merely an external behavior. It is what we actually are. Violence, cruelty, intolerance, hatred, ignorance, hypocrisy etc. are a few of the evils one should be free from for being gentle. A gentle person does not leave his goodness when he is hurt or harmed by others.

Serenity of mind is silence (**maun**) in this context. When dualities of happiness-sorrow, gain-loss, success-failure, victory—defeat etc. do not cause turbulent ripples in the mind, the mind can be said to be in silence.

Human mind has the property of not being stable even for a fraction of second. It keeps on roaming from here to there. It has the greatest speed among all the things that change their positions with time. A star may be many light years away from us but our mind can make a visit to the star and come back instantaneously. When we are able to concentrate on something for as long as we desire and can detach it from it at will, we can say we have control over our mind. We, as human beings are the most superior species on the earth and have extraordinary intelligence. It is said that we have intuitive power also.

We can make best use of our mind-intelligence faculty if we are able to learn how to control our mind. Geeta has used the word '**atmavinigraha**' for control over mind.

The last quality necessary for mental penance is freeing oneself from selfish thoughts and having nothing to do with pride and arrogance. If we possess these qualities we think of good and welfare of others. Geeta has used the word '**bhavasanshuddhi**' for this property, which literally means 'purity of feelings'.

This was about **mental penance**.

After describing penance of three types, the bodily penance, the vocal penance and the mental penance; Geeta classifies penance according to the values of its different classifications. The classifications are **Satvik**, the most valuable; **Rajas,** of ordinary value and the **Tamsik,** of no value and hence must be discarded. The three shlokas given hereunder describe the three classifications.

Shraddhaya paraya taptam tapastrividham naraiha,
Aphalakangshibhiha yuktaiha satvikam parichakshate.

It is the duty of the mankind to observe bodily, vocal and mental penance. One must observe them with **respect (shraddha)** and enthusiasm. All types of penance (bodily, vocal and mental) can come only under satvik (most valuable) penance. Satvik is most pious quality found in only those who are closest to the God. The shloka says that the penance of all the three types, bodily, vocal and mental when done with complete **shraddha** by human beings without desire of its fruits, i.e. selflessly is **satvik penance.** It becomes absolutely necessary to mention here; in the context of Gandhi; that the purpose behind the narration of Geeta (It is believed that Geeta was narrated by an incarnation of God), was for the benefit of the living beings, human beings in particular. Arjuna, the one who raised question was a human being and raised questions keeping his good in mind; and the God answered his questions in sufficient detail entertaining even cross questions. What we have discussed so far in the book and what more we shall discuss in pages ahead is likely to be very close and consistent with teachings of Geeta.

Most of us try to gain knowledge. Many of us turn to time tested wisdom of scriptures in quest of deeper knowledge. But, very rarely we find people in public life who try to practically use the wisdom that gives insight into the meaning and purpose of human life; for the benefit of the people. And out of them, those who commit to make themselves suffer endlessly, to see that humanity is benefitted are almost impossible to be found.

Is it possible for a human being to commit for a cause that demands everything; everything forever? Gandhi said;

> *What is impossible for human being is a child's play for the God. If we have faith in Him who decides the fate of the*

*minutest particle in this nature, all that
is impossible becomes possible. I am
spending my days with this last hope.*

(Mahatma Gandhi in England;
Mahadev Desai)

There are millions in this world who work very hard, go
though extreme hardships and make rare sacrifices. But,
behind their sacrifices are their desires; that is, ordinary
human desires. Ordinary human desires can be fulfilled,
sometimes, may be for a short while; but humanity hardly
gains anything when such desires are satisfied.

Perhaps it is the God, and the God alone, who wishes well
for all; that is animate or inanimate in His creation. If we
are parts of God, there is likelihood that we also possess
minds that think just as the God thinks. Then why it is
that the vast majority among us does not think the way
God thinks? Is it because that we do not have faith in our
abilities? Or, is it because that we ourselves are doubtful
about our intentions?

Did Gandhi have full faith in his intentions and his
abilities? I think; he had. He had because he had faith in
God.

**Satkar mana poojartham tapo dambhena cha aiva yat.
Kriyate tadiha proktam rajasam chalam adhruvam.**

When penance and austerities are performed hypocritically with the intention that one should be appreciated, praised, honoured, idolized or worshipped; then it is of ordinary value (**rajas**). Such penance can produce ordinary results some times. It is also doubtful that the results obtained through penance that is **rajas** in character would be lasting even to some extent.

Moodhagrahenatmano yat peedaya kriyate tapah,
Parasya utsadanartham va tat tamasam udahritam.

Penance that is performed with foolish intention that may cause injury to self or others is worthless and harmful (**tamsik**).

It is not possible to obtain positive results that benefit the people without making some sacrifices and suffering on part of those who intend and act for public welfare even when the level of evil that pervades in the society is not high.

At this juncture it becomes very important to understand and realize that, in the existing world, the evil and violence that one has to fight against is not distant from us. We do not easily find cruel and tyrannical rulers or invaders that snatch away our freedom. We have democracies. We exercise our right to select those who make policies for our benefit. We can make our voices heard. We can proceed to find relief against any injustice caused to us. Still, the humanity is being injured by the acts of human beings. Violence has come closer to us. We do not trust our neighbour the way we trusted him half of a century before. Is it not because, traditionally, the violence was answered with the help of violence? Are we at the verge of losing all hopes? Is it because of this that many of us are busy in seeking temporary pleasures and a few of us are trying to find solutions through **penance** that are **rajas** or **tamsik** in character?

Gandhi said;

> *The hardest heart and the grossest ignorance must disappear before rising sun of suffering without anger and without malice.*

(The Collected Works of Mahatma Gandhi)

He also said;

> *I do not get that disturbed to see people suffering, as I get when I have to see their downfall.*

(The Diary of Mahadev Desai; Editor, N.D. Parikh)

14

A SHORT PAUSE

My mantra is not Shri Ram; it is "Hey Ram".

(Bapu Ke Karavas Ki Kahani;
Dr. Sushila Nayyar)

In his autobiography Gandhi wrote about old family servant Rambha who taught him to use Ramanama for getting rid of his fears. In his prayers also he chanted, ". . . . patita pavan Sita Ram . . ." in Hindi and, " . . . peed parai jaane re . . ." in Gujrati.['Patit pavan' means, one who purifies the impure and 'peed parai jaane re' means, the one who understands the pains of others]. For Gandhi, God was merciful and caring for those who were weak, in pain or had fallen. When one says, "Hey Ram" or "Hey Bhagavan", he, in fact, begs for the mercy of the God.

I am like a puppet in the hand of God. He makes me dance and I dance the way He wants me to dance.

(The Diary of Mahadev Desai;
Editor, N.D. Parikh)

In all the fields, whether big or small, worshipping truth and non-violence is the only goal of my life.

**(The Diary of Mahadev Desai;
Editor, N.D. Parikh)**

Gandhi was committed to **truth**. Serving humanity selflessly was his method to realize the truth. **Non-violence** was the only way to remove all hurdles in the path of service, according to him. The task was not easy and could not have been achieved without the blessing and mercy of God. For Gandhi achieving **truth** through **non-violence** meant realizing **God** for eternal peace and happiness. That is what we focused on in the book so far.

Gandhi faced many arguments that attached great importance to goals and viewed means as secondary. Gandhi never agreed. Gandhi was prepared to forgo the fruits of his efforts if they were achieved through means that in his opinion were not right. He never wanted freedom for India if that was to be achieved through violence. Readers would recall that he did not spell 'kettle' correctly in his childhood, even when his teacher asked him to copy it from his neighbour's note-book.

He would not have sought emancipation unless he had explored the truth by serving the humanity selflessly. He could not have served humanity if means adopted for removing obstacles in the path had to be violent.

Let us think about the words **sadhya, sadhan, sadhana and sadhak** in this context. What one desires to achieve is **sadhya.** The effort one makes to achieve the **sadhya** is **sadhana.** The tools one chooses or the means one adopts to achieve the **sadhya** is **sadhan.** And the one who desires to realize some lofty ideals and makes efforts for it is called **sadhak.**

Gandhi often said man is not animal. What he meant was that a man needs to make efforts for achieving a few things in addition to keeping his body and soul together. Animals, instinctively, make only those efforts that are needed for their survival. Man, through his efforts, has to ensure that happiness prevails in this creation of the God, which for us is, this world. We all know that many find it difficult to survive in this world and hence are unhappy. Gandhi thought, as human beings it was our duty to make efforts to reduce sorrows of those who are unhappy. To do this, efforts are needed in two ways. First, we should not become a cause of others' sorrow. Second, we must try to eliminate, as far as possible, all that causes unhappiness.

Gandhi did not preach. He simply went ahead to do what he considered was right. He found that the job of making others happy, especially those who were weak and deprived in many respects, was not all that easy. He keenly observed his own shortcomings that caused hindrance in his efforts. He worked hard to get rid of his own shortcomings. He decided to fight. He fought with himself and he fought with his surroundings.

*A life without vows is like a ship without
an anchor or like an edifice that is built on
sand instead of solid rock.*

(Mahatma; D.G. Tendulkar)

Wherever he was and in whichever hour of the day he
was able to find a cause to pick up a fight, he picked up
a fight. He fought to stop a fight. He fought if salt was
taxed. He fought if a small pencil was being thrown away
by someone treating it to have become useless. He had his
own notions of right and wrong, but that were based on
what was said or written by those who had devoted their
lives for exploring the truth; those who were considered
to be the great men possessing true knowledge; the
knowledge that was for the good of the entire humanity.
Gandhi tried to gain that knowledge, internalized it and
ensured that it appealed to his own conscience. Gandhi
relied on a very small principle of life, that was, if we
commit ourselves totally for the good of others (one can,
more appropriately, use the word 'universe' instead of
'others') we can consider that our good is also being done
thereby. Conversely, if we keep ourselves at the centre of
all our efforts, we may cause harm to others; that in turn
would mean causing harm to the universe; and by virtue
of we being a part of universe, we would also be harmed.
That was Gandhi's truth. He clarified it sufficiently and
repeatedly.

Being a man of action Gandhi was noticed by others. He
was loved, liked, followed, criticized, hated, opposed,

forcefully prevented from moving on the path he had chosen and so on and so forth. Of course, Gandhi reacted. He reacted by reviewing his knowledge and modifying it with experiences gained through his work and actions; by filtering things through his conscience again; and by preparing himself to act again, that is, to fight again.

When Gandhi became a public figure his field of operation became very large. He needed support. He needed people who thought and worked more or less like him. He needed to communicate to them about his thoughts and about the methods to accomplish the identified tasks. He wrote and spoke; and above all he worked himself. That formed the major part of the material from where we can know about Gandhi.

We find that he spoke about and wrote about even the minutest of the details of thoughts and the action-reaction matrices that existed and were continuously proliferating. New goals (**sadhya**) were to be targeted; new methods to operate (**sadhan**) had to be thought of; and those who were to operate for achieving them (**sadhak**) needed to be provided appropriate **skills** and **detailed guidance.** The **sadhan** had to be **non-violent** and **selfless action.** Gandhi never compromised on that. All what I wrote about **non-violence, shraddha, humility and self respect, courage, forgiveness and penance** was part of what Gandhi was trying to advise those who worked for his ideals, supported him or followed him. I have endeavoured to explain the qualities Gandhi emphasized on; in my own words but taking sufficient care to restrict to only that literature that Gandhi had referred to as having studied. I have also taken care of innovations, if any, made by Gandhi in knowledge existing in such literature. For example, Gandhi solicited non-violence very strictly whereas Geeta is strict about Dharma. I have allowed Gandhi's view to prevail because Dharma allows modifications according to time, place and circumstances.

I am concentrating on what Gandhi thought. I found that Gandhi was remarkably consistent in his thoughts, speech and action. I am aware of a few criticisms about inconsistency in his thoughts and actions. I have preferred to keep myself away from some of them, that I found not to be very relevant for furthering our objective, that is, to see whether Gandhi's views are useful and practically implementable. Incidentally, most of the criticisms about inconsistencies arise because of lack of depth in knowledge of the critics or improper attention paid by them to the context.

A few qualities that a **sadhak** must acquire according to Gandhi viz. freedom from enmity and anger, simplicity, absence of greed, patience, peace, strong desire to gain knowledge etc. shall be taken up after this pause. After that we shall discuss in what way he visualized a better human society. By that time we would have known Gandhi to quite some extent and would be ready to discuss whether Gandhi's existence had been of some serious consequence for the world.

I thought it fit to insert this 'pause' after 13 chapters so that I am able to synchronize my thoughts with that of my readers.

> *It is not wise to ask what we can accomplish . . . I can only say that please try to think about the principles I have presented before you and have seriously tried to put them into practice; and please try to adopt them in your life; then God will help you in finding the paths you have been looking for.*

**(Bapu Ke Karavas Ki Kahani;
Dr. Sushila Nayyar)**

15

SELF-LEARNING

The food one is not able to digest is of no use. Similarly, the thoughts that are not digested have no use. Accepting things with intellect but without internalizing them is a kind of indigestion.

Indigestion of thoughts and knowledge is worse than indigestion of food. Indigestion of food can be cured but indigestion of thoughts cannot be cured.

**(Gandhi Seva Sangh;
Hudali, 04.16.1937)**

The thought of truth and non-violence cannot be circulated through books. One live example is always more meaningful than crores of books. Books do not have life. Books may be written . . . . But they cannot become the right tool **(sadhan)** *for us. Satyagrahi* **(the one who insists on truth)** *grows by adopting the principles of truth and putting them into practice.*

**(Gandhi Seva Sangh;
Vrindavan, 05.03.1939)**

*Action and knowledge, without devotion,
are cold and dry and many of them even
become shackles.*

(The Collected Works of Mahatma Gandhi)

This chapter hardly relates to the views Gandhi had on education. This chapter basically deals with the importance Gandhi attached to strong desire one must have and the assiduous efforts he must make, especially if he is a **sadhak**, for self development. Ancient Indian scriptures have given great importance to **Swadhyaya** (the process of gaining knowledge through one's own efforts). Many spiritual leaders have defined **Swadhyaya** as regular efforts one must make for studying **shastras** (scriptures) and other books, with intent and content to provide useful knowledge on philosophy of human life. According to my understanding, Gandhi gave little importance to this definition; instead of this, he appeared to be fairly close to the concept of **"Swasya adhyayah (adhyayanam) swadhyayah"**, which means self-study of root causes of one's own nature and behavior is **swadhyaya**.

Gandhi was never much in favour of bookish knowledge. Here one should not hurriedly conclude that Gandhi was against knowledge of sciences, languages, philosophy etc. He favoured, rather insisted upon, application of knowledge gained, for a right purpose; putting it into practice truthfully and devotedly; with a view to making that knowledge as one's own. Here the words 'truthfully and devotedly' are very important. Firstly, there cannot be any compromise regarding the tools (**sadhan**) that are to be used when one is putting knowledge gained into practice. Secondly, one must have **shraddha** in the task one is performing. In simple language one should be devoted to the task in hand, he should love doing it and should not treat it as drudgery. When one tries to accomplish a task in aforesaid manner; he would realize that he, subconsciously or involuntarily, goes through a process of introspection; that helps him to watch himself in action as well as makes him aware of the fine points, essence and intent of the knowledge, which is being applied for accomplishment of the task in hand.

We often find, that the quality of same job performed by two different individuals of equal calibre, differ. The reason behind this is that the two differ in their devotion and true understanding of the task performed.

> *I told you something and you have accepted it; that is not enough. Worshipping other human being is not our job. Only ideals and principles deserve to be worshipped . . . Do not worship me. There is truth, that may be worshipped. There is non-violence, that may be worshipped. The thing you have internalized* **(learned and practiced with devotion)** *becomes fully yours. Only*

those things, for which you do not have to depend on others, are actually yours.

(Gandhi Seva Sangh; Hudali, 04.16.1937)

Stuffing one's mind with useless knowledge and information is worthless. Knowledge that takes us away from things that God expects from us, are useless. The practice of accumulating useless knowledge must be abandoned.

(Yarvada Jail, Madhya Pradesh, 08.26.1930)

Gandhi usually spoke and wrote about the tasks that were to be performed and about the caution that must be exercised in performing them. It becomes somewhat difficult to sift out his views on science of learning to accomplish a task. However, it is clear that the elements he laid emphasis on were the nature and quality of tasks; the tools that must be adopted in performing those tasks; and the care that must be taken when the tasks are being performed. For him service to humanity was the task worth performing and while serving others, one must be least concerned about his self interests. In other words the component of sacrifice was important in Gandhi's views. Gandhi was aware that if not causing harm is the essence of truth; then, some may think of minimizing actions to avoid causing harm. He did not appreciate the idea of inaction propagated by many spiritualists. For serving others one had to act and when there was an action hindrance were bound to appear. The action-reaction relationships and obstacles associated therewith were expected to occur in the process of service. Gandhi insisted that each and every action must become non-violent to uphold the principles of causing no harm. He vigorously came out with arguments, one after the other, in defense of non-violence.

In this context, when we think about the process of learning that was necessary for performance of tasks that Gandhi and his followers must have had before them, a feeling of insufficiency and inadequacy sets in. I often found worry and desperation in Gandhi's words, while he made repeated appeals to people for sticking to truth and non-violence. This desperation was more visible in late stages of Gandhi's life. After returning to India from South Africa, Gandhi realized that a very big responsibility awaited him. Soon he gathered that problems were more than what he had ever imagined, both in quantum and in nature. Worst part of it was that they were interrelated. Gandhi's simplicity, straightforwardness and reputation of his work in South Africa, won him many followers. They were very enthusiastic and were in great hurry. While Gandhi was aware that non-violence is a matter of great courage, self-improvement, **swadhyaya**, sacrifice and enormous patience; his followers were surcharged with impatient hope. Gandhi visualized the great potential but in a raw state. Gandhi knew that if his experiments succeeded it will be a service, not only to his country but to the entire humanity. He knew that he hardly had the time, the time that God alone could grant. He prayed and continued with his experiments.

> *The world outside Champaran was not known to them. And yet they received me as though we had been age-old friends. It is no exaggeration, but the literal truth, to say that in this meeting with peasants I was face to face with God, Ahimsa and Truth.*

**(My Experiments with Truth;
M.K. Gandhi, Chapter 6, Part V)**

Glimpses, of his views on learning are very relevant in relation to education. While I will discuss Gandhi on education later in the book, I consider it necessary to include a part of it here because of the inherent similarity in education and self-learning.

What Gandhi meant by learning, cannot be understood unless we do not discuss in brief some portions of Chapters 11 and 12 of Part IV of his autobiography. In South Africa Gandhi was instrumental in establishing a very modest farm; drawing inspiration from Ruskin's *Unto This Last.* He named it *Tolstoy Farm.* He says in Chapter 11 referred above titled as '*As Schoolmaster*';

> *. . . it was found necessary to make some provision for the education of its boys*

and girls . . . . Indian teachers were scare, and even when available, none would be ready to go to a place 21 miles distant from Johannesburg on a small salary . . . . I did not believe in the existing system of education, and I had in mind to find out by experience and experiment the true system. Only this much I knew that, under ideal conditions, true education could be imparted only by parents . . . Tolstoy Farm was a family, in which I occupied the place of the father . . . .

I had always given the first place to the culture of heart . . . I regarded character building as the proper foundation for their education, and if the foundation was firmly laid, I was sure that the children could learn all the other things themselves or with the assistance of friends.

In Chapter 12, Part IV titled as *Literary Training*, Gandhi says;

I had undertaken to teach Tamil and Urdu. The little Tamil I knew was acquired during voyages and in jail. I had not gone beyond Pope's Excellent Tamil handbook. My knowledge of the Urdu script was all that I had acquired on a single voyage and my knowledge of the language was confined to the familiar Persian and Arabic words that I had learnt from contacts with Mussalman friends . . . .

Such was the capital with which I had to carry on. In poverty of literary equipment my colleagues went one better than I. But my love for the languages of my country, my confidence in my capacity as a teacher, as also the ignorance of my pupils, and more than that, their generosity, stood me in good stead.

The Tamil boys were all born in South Africa . . . did not know the script at all. So I had to teach them the script and rudiments of grammar. That was easy enough. My pupils knew that they could any day beat me in Tamil conversation . . . . when Tamilians not knowing English, came to see me, they became my interpreters. I got along merrily because I never attempted to disguise my ignorance from my pupils.

Therefore in spite of my colossal ignorance of the language I never lost their love and respect . . . Mussalman boys knew the script. I had to simply stimulate in them an interest in reading and to improve their handwriting.

These youngsters were for the most part unlettered and unschooled. But I found . . . had very little to teach them, beyond weaning them away from their laziness . . . .

Of text books, about which we hear so much, . . . I did not find it at all necessary to load the boys with quantities of books . . . I remember very little that my teachers taught from books, but I have even now a clear recollection of the things they taught me independently of the books.

Children take in much more and with less labour through their ears than through their eyes . . . . Reading was a task for them, but listening to me was a pleasure, when I did not bore them by failure to make my subject interesting.

Although I have not covered the aspects of physical work and play by the children of *Tolstoy Farm* in the above quotations, I can say that Gandhi's views on self-learning were sufficiently tilted towards observation, listening and participating in physical work instead of reading of books.

We can say; knowing through observation, listening and participation; experiencing and experimenting with real life situations; and finally continuous introspection; are most important elements of learning. Gandhi did not undermine importance of books and other material but he was for human to human relationship; that is evident. To extend Gandhi's views, I may say that Gandhi would have never welcomed audio-visual media as an alternative to books because it cannot replace real-life experiencing.

16

ABSENCE OF ENMITY AND ANGER

No man could look upon another as his enemy unless he first became his own enemy.

(Mahatma; D.G. Tendulkar)

True ahimsa should mean a complete freedom from ill-will and anger and hate and an overflowing love for all.

(Mahatma; D.G. Tendulkar)

Is it possible that Mr. X considers Mr. Y as his enemy and Mr. Y does not consider Mr. X as his enemy? The most negative answer we can get would be, "Very unlikely but not absolutely impossible." If I am permitted to sound a little ridiculous, I would put another question, "What kind of enmity can be called ideal enmity?" If I say, when two mutual enemies have equal desire to harm each other and are equally afraid of each other; that could be called ideal enmity. If for the time being, we leave aside many other negative emotions like hatred, malice, anger, cruelty, arrogance etc. that come in package form with enmity; we find that desire to harm the enemy and fear of being harmed by the enemy; only these two remain in a pair. As long as this pair exists, enmity persists.

Those who are locked in a relationship of enmity, two people, two groups or two nations; invariably make all possible efforts to maintain the status quo. They hire people to defend themselves, they buy and maintain arms and from time to time make open demonstrations to show that they have enough strength to answer any attempt of violence against them. They are compelled to invest valuable resources of time, money and energy available with them to avoid any harm that may be caused by their enemy. They lose opportunities that they could have otherwise availed of if the enmity had ended. Is it not a definite kind of loss of freedom for each of them? That is what Gandhi said that no one could become enemy of another without becoming his own enemy.

> *Violence cannot be destroyed with bigger violence. This is a natural law.*

(Harijan Sevak; 03.30.1947)

If one tries to end animosity by causing harm to his enemy to an extent that the enemy becomes weak enough not to remain a threat any further; even then the problem remains unsolved. The thought of enmity would not die and may raise its head to take revenge. It does not need any elaboration. Almost all of us are fully aware of some kind of hateful relationships that exist between nations, races or ethnic groups. Behind each such relationship there must have been a history of violence. Those who have studied Thermodynamics know that entropy once created can never be destroyed and the nature has to bear its burden. The same applies to violence. Gandhi said;

> *You need two people to initiate a fight. One cannot clap with one hand. But friendship can be initiated from one side. One must know that friendship is not a transaction. The other name for friendship is non-violence or love. Friendship is not an act of cowards. It is an act of the courageous and the farsighted.*

(Harijan Sevak; 08.03.1947)

Gandhi said this on 25th July 1947, about 20 days before India became free from British rule. The statement of Gandhi had a bearing on his anguish about division of India that was impending. There was much communal violence in many parts of the then undivided India. The violence has not ended even after 66 years.

About nine hundred years back India was invaded with intentions of loot and plunder. Later people from other lands identifying themselves as belonging to a different religion forcibly ruled India. Those invaders had not come to spread their religious thoughts and beliefs in India, they had come to forcibly enjoy the fruits of resources that India had in plenty. It is only because it was a violent act that religious and communal harmony still remains disturbed in India. As against this, an Indian emperor Ashoka, after a fierce battle that he had won, decided to shun violence and sent his people with specific purpose to spread Buddhism in other parts of the world and we do not find any violence existing on that account.

> Opposition is not necessarily enmity; it is merely misused and made an occasion for enmity.

Sigmund Freud

Violence begets violence and nothing else. Gandhi was uncompromising on non-violence.

To get rid of enmity the only option is to make your enemy believe that he should not be afraid of you. But to do this you must kill the thought of harming him. Again, that cannot be done unless you are courageous enough to take a risk and prepared to stick to non-violence even if your enemy tries to harm you. There are enough reasons to believe that such risks are worth taking.

> *All miracles that have occurred till date in this world have been caused by actions of unknown forces that act silently but very effectively. Non-violence is the most unknown and most effective of them all.*

(Harijan Sevak; 03.27.1937)

There is nothing invisible and unknown in violence. As against this non-violence is seventy-five percent invisible and unknown. It, therefore, becomes difficult to deal with it. When non-violence becomes active it comes to the forefront with a great speed and suddenly becomes visible. By the time it becomes fully known the war is over and non-violence wins.

(Harijan Sewak; 03.27.1937)

The best way to understand Gandhi's view on enmity is to refer to the following Sutra from Patanjali, who made a very significant contribution to ancient Indian philosophy.

Ahimsa pratishthayam tat-sannidhau vaira-tyagah.

[Translation: When the principle of non-violence is very firmly settled in one all enmity around him withers away. Meaning: Non-violence can be considered as firmly settled only when one's thoughts, actions and conduct all become non-violent. He should not have any kind of violence; whether it is mental, vocal or bodily. The **sutra** suggests that such person would think, act and behave in a manner that all that is violent in and around him is converted into non-violence. Absolute non-violence is **satvik** (extraordinarily pure and influential) in nature. Its current is unstoppable.

Some learned people have explained that no one is actually free from external influences. They have said that if two people, both violent in nature, came face to face even with a trivial point of discord; there is a high probability of their becoming enemies of each other. This enmity would be lasting because; both will receive more violence from each other in addition to what they had prior to the seeding of enmity between the two. As against this if an individual with violent nature and the other with non-violent nature encounter each other with a point of discord; both would influence each other with their respective strengths of their natures, violent and non-violent. If non-violence of the non-violent is poor in strength, there is much likelihood that non-violent would also become violent. But, if the non-violent one is firmly settled in non-violence, then he will win and may convert the violent into non-violent. One should not overlook that pure non-violence is **satvik** in nature whereas violence could be **rajas** or **tamsik**. We know **satvik** is superior, more commanding and piercingly influential.]

Before closing the topic of enmity I wish to say that enmity between two individuals or two families may not cause that much harm as it could be caused by enmity between two groups, sects, the followers of two religions or two nations.

> *If elementary conditions necessary for establishing peace are not followed; it is impossible to establish peace. If the respected leaders of human race who think*

of controlling use of arms decide to stop their use completely then peace can be established.

(Harijan Sevak; 05.23.1936)

We exist in all others and all exist within us. If we have this feeling we will not be angry. Sea consists of many drops; that have their separate identities and they are the sea also.

(The Diary of Mahadev Desai;
Editor, N.D. Parikh)

Devil is not an entity. It is a principle of denying truth. Accepting truth is Divine. The divine gives us life. It is life. It is Brahma.

Denial of truth has no life. Sometimes, even dead bodies falsely appear to have life. That is illusion. Some get deceived and run after this illusion.

(Bapu Ke Karavas Ki Kahani;
Dr. Sushila Nayyar)

When many go after the illusions, often they find them crossing each other's path. The fear of losing things, because of others, generates anger. One may fear loss of objects one is attached to or loss of his false pride and prestige. When one gets angry he may be inclined to cause harm to the one which he considers as the one responsible for loss or possible loss. This, however, is secondary. Before causing harm to the individual considered as responsible for the possible loss; one who is angry causes harm to himself. Geeta says;

Dhyayto vishayan punsah sangateshu upjayate;
Sangat sanjayte kamah, kamat krodhah abhijayate.
Krodhat bhavati sammohah, sammohat smritivibhramah;
Smritibhranshad buddhinashah, buddhinashat pranashyati.

(Geeta; Chapter II, shloka 62&63)

[Meaning: Attachment towards illusionary things causes desires for their possession. When there is some obstruction in fulfillment of such desires, there arises anger. An angry individual loses ability to distinguish the right from the wrong. This causes confusion in the mind. Confusion in mind causes harm to man's ability to reason out properly. When the ability of reasoning is damaged it causes downfall of man.]

If we deeply contemplate, we find that sensory desires, attachments, greed and anger; all the four reduce the ability to distinguish right from wrong; then why is it that anger may become the biggest cause of downfall of man? It is because that an angry man does not remain that much concerned about his own welfare, as he becomes more concerned about causing harm to the one, who in his opinion is the cause of his anger. An angry man is always more vulnerable to any harm than the one who is not angry.

This exactly is the reason why we say that an angry person lands himself in trouble before he can cause harm to others.

> *If we lose confidence in anybody or some misunderstanding is developed between him and us, it is our duty to approach him for clarification. Bible tells us two things in this matter. The first is, "Approach your opponent as quickly as possible for making a compromise." The second is, "If you develop a feeling of anger against someone, do not wait for sunset for sorting out the issue that caused anger."*

> *In matters of policy, words of Bible or any religious scripture must be considered as final.*

> **(Gandhi Seva Sangh; Vrindavan, 05.05.1939)**

17

KINDNESS, CHARITY & SACRIFICES

The only way the God can have courage to appear before hungry and unemployed to fulfill their wishes; is to grant them work and promise them wages for their work; in lieu of food.

I cannot think of insulting, those who are naked for want of clothes; by giving them such clothes in charity that are not needed by them. I will never commit the sin of trying to become the provider and savior to those who are poor, knowing full well that I also have a hand in bringing them to this predicament.

I will never ever think of offering them leftover food from my plate or the clothes that I have worn. I will prefer to do physical work with them and share my food with them. I will give them proper place in society.

(Harijan Sevak; 02.25.1939)

The feeling generated in one; to help others whom he finds in difficulty or in pain, for making them get rid of their pain and removing their difficulties; is called kindness.

The God looks after the welfare of His creation. Sometimes He does certain acts that appear to us as difficulties, but they actually are meant to make us learn what needs to be learned. We are recipients of God's grace as well as kindness. God's will is only for the benefit of His creation. The fact is that we cannot understand God's will. It is beyond us. It is enough for us if we attribute whatever good is possible for the entire universe to the God, because that alone can inspire us and help us in leading a meaningful life.

The case of ordinary person is entirely different. If he is kind; he 'thinks' that 'he' is kind. This actually implies that he thinks that there may be others who are not kind enough. When an ordinary person 'gives', he does it to receive 'the thought of having done the good', that is, the thought that makes him happy. Saintly people make rigorous efforts to minimize the sense of 'doership'.

The one who serves the people is neither elated by praises nor is he depressed by criticism. Real praise for the servant of people is his service only.

(Harijan Sevak; 09.22.1046)

*Public service if selflessly done is like
walking on the edge of a sword. If one is
ready to collect praise for it, why should
he hide his face if he is criticized?*

**(Satyagraha in South Africa; M.K.
Gnadhi)**

First of all let us see if there is a relation between the
qualities of kindness as referred and explained by
scriptures or in different religious books; and the concept
of service Gandhi had. 'People' for Gandhi primarily
meant the human beings who suffer due to the harm
caused by man. For Gandhi causing harm was a negation
of truth by some untruth or violence. To uphold truth is
the sacred responsibility, the duty or Dharma for human
beings. Here, one need not 'feel' the suffering of others
for initiating an effort to help someone in getting rid of
his pains. In this case the continued incidence of suffering
of some or many is 'felt' so persistently that it becomes
a practical knowledge. The **sadhak** has that knowledge
and is capable of imagining the pain with or without an
external stimulant. His kindness is not the type of kindness
ordinary people have. It is type of kindness saintly people
have. Saintly people are not puppets of their emotions.
They develop a natural kindheartedness and their thoughts
and actions are governed by it all the time without
involvement of emotions or desires. This is a state one
can achieve when one is able to exercise control over his
desires, mind and intellect. The **sadhak** becomes **aware**
of what is happening and how he is supposed to act by

remaining detached from fruits of his action. The one who attains this state is called **sthitaprajna**.

Geeta says;

Prajahati yada Kaman sarvan Parth manogatan; Atmani aiva atmana tushtah sthitaprajna tada uchyate.

(Geeta; Chapter II, shloka 55)

[Translation: When one completely abandons all the desires that arise in his mind and he settles with full contentment within him, he then is called **sthitaprajna** (one with unwavering intellect)]

A **sadhak**, has to have enormous kindheartedness, but that should have become his nature. His own mind and intellect should not be affected by external stimulants of pain and sorrow in a manner that could affect his emotions to distract him from his duties that he has become committed to. We know that **sadhak's** duty (**Dharma**) is to selflessly serve the humanity so that sorrows and pains caused to it are minimized. We can say that a **sadhak** acquires single-mindedness towards the **sadhan** that he possesses to perform his duties effectively.

The strength of an armed soldier lies in his gun or his sword. Take them away, he would become helpless. But the one, who has truly understood non-violence, has the strength granted by the God to him.

(Harijan Sevak; 11.26.1939)

In the above statement Gandhi says that whereas **sadhan** of an armed soldier is his gun or sword, a non-violent **sadhak** relies on the strength granted by the God to him. What is that strength God has granted him?

Non-violence is the best possible active force. This is the inner strength of the man. The God is within us; it is His strength that we make use of when we have internalized what non-violence is.

(Harijan Sevak; 11.19.1938)

Kindheartedness, Charity and Sacrifice are interconnected topics. While we have discussed so far about **sadhak** and **sadhan** to build a deeper understanding of Gandhi's thinking process with respect to kindheartedness we may now go to **sadhya** (the thing to be achieved).

Here I have used the word 'sacrifice' to mean Sanskrit word 'Yajna'. *Yajna* is not a thought or quality. It is an action. Some ancient kings performed *yajna* for the good and welfare of their people; others did it to enhance their influence as kings. Here we will not use *yajna* in ritualistic sense, through which one tries to please the Gods so that actions proposed to be performed become hurdle free. Gandhi thought that 'truth is God' and our duty in this life is to realize truth. If we stick to truth, the God shall always be with us; hence there was no necessity to perform any ritual to obtain God's blessings; that is what Gandhi believed in.

> *Yajna having come to us with our birth, we are debtors all our lives. And thus forever bound to serve the universe.*

(Geeta Bodh; M.K.Gandhi)

From the day we are conceived the external world puts in many efforts and thereby goes through many hardships and pains so that we survive and grow. Those who help us to live in this world; may be known to us or they may be unknown; they may be still living when we are there or they may have died even centuries before our birth. For example, when we are in the process of getting education as students, the knowledge we get in a fraction of second might have been created thousands of years ago, through the persistent exploratory efforts of many. Some of them might have even sacrificed their lives for creating that knowledge. That is why, as Gandhi says, "We are debtors all our lives."

To repay our debt we have to serve the universe throughout our lives. And that service has to be without expecting anything in return from the world. That is self-less service. That is **Yajna,** our immediate **sadhya** which becomes **sadhan** to realize the **truth**.

> *Yajna is duty to be performed, or service to be rendered, all twenty four hours of the day.*

(The Mind of Mahatma Gandhi; Prabhu & Rao)

> *The service that does not please the heart of the one who serves is not pleasing to the one who is being served. All comforts of life and wealth become insignificant against the pleasure of selfless service.*

(My Experiments with Truth; M.K. Gandhi)

> *On the basis of my experiences I have developed a belief that if one is absolutely selfless in his service; sadhan and sadhak appear, from somewhere or the other, in times of difficulties.*

(My Experiments with Truth; M.K. Gandhi)

The last quotation has no logical explanation. Geeta has referred about the enormous strength of **Nishkam Karma.**

[An action without the desire of its fruit; Geeta has also described it as an action whose fruits are surrendered to the God.] Perhaps, it is because of the Supreme power who exists and governs the universe, and whose strength becomes active at the right occasion and at the right time. It can only be experienced by those who serve the needy without any self interest. I have discussed *yoga* in the ultimate chapter of this book. Perhaps, that would explain the phenomenon Gandhi is referring to.

> *Every single act of one, who would lead*
> *a life of purity, should be in the nature of*
> *yajna.*

(Geeta Bodh; M. K. Gandhi)

It seems the word 'charity' was non-existent in the dictionary of Gandhi. The very first quotation given in this chapter confirms this. It is believed that Swami Vivekananda used an expression Daridra Narayan for the poor. Daridra means poor and Narayan is used for God. I do not think Vivekananada thought of this word because this is found in literature written on the basis of ancient Indian scriptures in simple language and in form of stories with a view to conveying the ideals of scriptures to the common and not so learned people, popularly known as *puranas*. In fact Indian mythology sees God in everything that must be served by man. Ancient Indian thinkers saw God in useful trees and plants, rivers, in some animals, fire, earth and similarly the poor. Gandhi adopted this expression and believed in it. Similarly, Gandhi invariably used the expression 'Harijan' (God's person) for those people who were considered to be belonging to low castes. How can one give charity to God? Those who believe in God, serve him.

Was Gandhi against charity? My answer is, "Yes, he was." He was against charity because it has a sense of 'giver-ship'. Gandhi was in favour of giving one's life away, when needed, while serving humanity or the needy but not charity (*dan* is the Sanskrit word for charity) because it is difficult to make it a humble act. Even if one gives without any knowledge to anybody (not even the receiver), the giver will always be aware of his 'good act'. Charity for the cause of service was acceptable to Gandhi because that became a 'service' to the cause of service. There again he preferred **shramdan** (charity in form of physical labour). Let us see what Geeta has to say about **satvik dan** (most superior and pious charity).

Datavyam iti yat danam deeyate anupakarine,
Deshe kale cha patre cha tat danam satvikam smritam.

(Geeta, Chapter XVII, Shloka 20)

[Translation: Charity that is given away considering it as one's duty, without any selfish desires only to the one who deserves to receive charity according to the demands of the country (place) and time provided the receiver has neither done any favour to the giver in past nor he is doing any favour to the giver at present and it is also unlikely that he would be doing any favour to the giver in future.]

We have discussed about the demerits of 'giver-ship' and that of selfish intent behind charity but there is a need to understand what Geeta says about the favour having been done, being done or likely to be done by the receiver to the giver. Often those who serve us do things without any consideration of a return there against. If we give them something as 'gift' on certain occasions, viewing it as charity, it is not charity. Gandhi spoke about our indebtedness to the universe. How can one give charity to anybody in this world? The poor are poor today just because our ancestors deprived them of what was rightfully due to them. Is the act of extending charity to them can be classified as **satvik dan?** Gandhi, indeed, did not have the word 'charity' in his dictionary.

18

APARIGRAHA AND ASTEYA

'Parigraha' means collecting and storing. One who is in search of truth and is non-violent does not collect and store. God does not store anything. We must have faith that we will get what we need every day.

If all follow this, there shall not be any shortages. A pauper wants to become a millionaire; a millionaire wants to become a billionaire. No one is satisfied. Poor has a right to feed him. It is the duty of the society that this right is not infringed upon and he gets his needful.

The rich must take lead for ensuring this. It is good for the both. Those who have enough must not aspire for more. They should not store further. This will ensure that those who do not have get what is rightfully theirs. In fact, both must learn the lesson of contentment.

. . . Good civilization does not aim at increasing the tendency of storing

(amassing wealth). It aims at not only reducing the tendency of amassing wealth but also discouraging the thought of indiscriminate storing and amassing wealth. More and more one tries to reduce the thought of storing; not only he becomes more satisfied in true sense but also gains by developing spirit of service in him. It is simply a matter of practice. It is the key for happy and healthy life with contentment and peace.

(Yarvada Jail; Madhya Pradesh, 08.26.1930)

Mantra One and Mantra Two of Ishopanishad, quoted in Chapter 03 emphasize the thought of refraining from the tendency of unnecessary storing and collection. What is behind this thought?

There may be a simple fear of, "What would happen tomorrow if I do not store?" We should seek an answer from the point of view of an ordinary human being and not that of a saint. Let us take the case of an ordinary farmer who stores food grains for his consumption till the next harvest at least; and if possible more, for if the next crop fails he would have something to bank upon. Is it not justified? Some spiritualist may say that nothing is certain in this life so why worry. But, God does not want that we should go hungry. It is true that nothing is certain. Using a truth to suppress another truth may be convenient but it is definitely inconsistent spiritually. It is circulating untruth, knowingly or unknowingly. It is against Dharma.

This may also happen that the same farmer finds that storing food grains even for two crop seasons is not sufficient because after all, there could be a risk of crop failure in third season also. If this farmer, to avoid such risk, stealthily encroaches into nearby farms of other farmers; so that he could have more food grains to store; shall we treat this farmer as one who acted with greater sense of responsibility towards his family? On the face of it, most of us would not consider the act of this farmer appropriate. However, the fact remains that most of us are directly or indirectly involved in similar acts. When we say that, to lead a better life we have to be more practical; we give ourselves a license to be unfair.

The third kind of farmer may be more inclined than others towards more comforts, more sensory pleasures, higher status in the society etc. He may adopt violent methods to encroach upon the rights of other farmers for satisfying his desires. After having amassed wealth much greater than others he may 'buy' support of weaker farmers around him to continue fulfilling his ever increasing desires with minimum efforts. Undoubtedly, there shall not be many who would like him. But, there shall be some who would envy him and would like to copy his ways and methods to become like him. His clan will proliferate. This also is happening in our society and we are also, more or less, a part of it.

We are never sure when some greed becomes our necessity and when some luxury becomes our need.

Gandhi did not preach about greed like many spiritual leaders do. In his heart he was in favour of equality of all human beings and an egalitarian social order but he preferred a path whereby people themselves realize where the truth lies and sought the ideal willingly, through their own non-violent efforts. He was aware that friction dissipates energy and makes the right movement all the more difficult. He was also aware that if the efforts were violent the failure was inevitable, today or tomorrow.

> *I fully agree that all that exists on this earth belong to people who live there. The difference is that they (the socialists and the communists) think all of us start together. I say all of us, individually, must start together, that is; we must immediately initiate brining about changes in our individual conducts. If we have faith in what we propagate we must begin with our own properties. They want to enforce it through law. But, law will put pressure. It means they cannot do it themselves. They are helpless.*

> **(Gandhi Sevak Sangh; Savali, 03.04.1936)**

The socialists want that all must think what they (the socialists) want them to think. There is no scheme in their mind about changing the thoughts and conduct of people.

This is not the path of non-violence. We have to work for bringing about changes in individual conduct of people. I do not say that I need an army to do it. I say that we must start immediately.

(Gandhi Seva Sangh; Delang, 03.26.1938)

I honour individual freedom. But we must remember that basically human being is a social being. He has reached in the present state of advancement by moulding his individual personality according to the needs of the society. Unbridled individualism is the law of wild animals. We have learned to balance individual freedom with social restraints.

(Harijan Sevak; 05.27.1939)

Gandhi had enormous confidence in human beings and humanity. That is why he preferred to be very patient about man's own greatest enemy, greed, which the man finds very difficult to get rid of. Gandhi said;

There is nothing wrong if one becomes good because of the pressure of circumstances. But if one becomes good for the sake of good it is better.

(Harijan Sevak; 11.12.1938)

Man is not at peace with himself till he has become like unto God.

(Geeta Bodh; M.K. Gandhi)

Whatever Gandhi could do in his life time was due to his untiring honest efforts and his faith in humanity. What he could do, cannot be considered as small by any stretch of imagination. Perhaps, we can find many who worked day and night with a missionary zeal that matches with that of Gandhi, but it is difficult to find one who had complete faith in humanity and worked on a canvass as big as that of Gandhi's. History has many examples when many became united to give a big jolt to greed of a few. But, there is no case when many decided to shake themselves off their own individual greed. Gandhi had this in mind. He worked for it also. There were obstacles in carrying out this experiment. His life time was consumed in handling those obstacles. It is unfortunate that Gandhi's work came to an abrupt halt after his death.

No one approves of theft. But Gandhi's views on theft go much wider and deeper. The quality of non-theft has been referred as **asteya** in ancient Indian scriptures. Gandhi wrote about this when he was in jail. I find it better to quote the essence of what he wrote. All the quotes given hereunder are from what Gandhi wrote in **Yarvada Jail, Madhya Pradesh** on **08.19.1930.**

> *While taking away things belonging to others without permission of the owner is, undoubtedly theft, sometimes using our own things without the knowledge of others who have a moral right on them is also theft.*

For example, if a father uses disproportionate part of his income for himself that cause hardships to his children, it may be considered as theft. Similarly, when many grown up children who earn well, thanks to sacrifices made by their parents for helping and supporting their growth, do not take care of their parents in their old age; that is also theft.

> *If one takes away something he does not need; from others in owner's knowledge and even with owner's permission; that also is theft. Things not needed by us should not be taken away from others.*

> *Looking at things with greed; with a desire of possessing them; not belonging to us is also theft. It is mental theft. In this case it is only greed, that is present initially but that can get converted into action in*

future, hence it is theft. The very thought of possessing something that one has not earned with his own labour is dangerous. He may try to get it by hook or by crook and at some stage that would become theft. Likewise there is theft of thoughts. People present ideas and thoughts of others as if they were owned by them, for enhancing their prestige; this is also theft. False pride is the culprit when theft of thoughts and ideas is committed.

The one who observes 'asteya' has to be very humble, careful and thoughtful. He must lead a simple life.

The worst thing about **greed** and **theft,** most of the time, is that they appear as innocent conducts, causing none or insignificant harm to others and if not checked in initial stages, they assume alarming proportions.

19

SIMPLICITY AND SELF-DISCIPLINE

Simplicity is the essence of universality.

(Mind of Mahatma Gandhi;
Prabhu & Rao)

All that is completely free of whatever is ostensible and frivolous is simple. Something cannot be made to 'appear' simple. It has to be simple. In the entire universe do we have anything which exists just for the sake of appearance? One can pick up anything from the nature that he could think as useless; some scientist would be able to explain how important it is and why? No one can tell exactly, how much about our own planet we know and how much of it still remains unknown. If we do not know enough it is our shortcoming. All that we have taken centuries to know, will take many more centuries to know or perhaps will never be able to know; must be very simple for the Creator of the universe. Complications arise only when one is not able to comprehend something. Even for a small child, the chapter he has understood is simple and the one he has not understood is difficult or complicated.

If we go to a grain merchant in a village to buy wheat, the merchant points to a gunny bag to show what he has for sale and tells the price.

Things that are highly priced or are not of right quality need much of good packaging, smart sales talk or attractive schemes. This is another aspect of simplicity. Whatever is genuine is simple.

Many spend hours to dress up when they go out to attend a function, but they leave their house in fraction of a second if there is a big fire in the house. They come out of their houses with whatever they are wearing because they know how important the life is. When we understand the real meaning and purpose of our life we shun all ostentation and frivolousness.

> It has been found that if we increase our needs in life our thought and conduct suffer. Contentment is the source of happiness. One who is always dissatisfied irrespective of what he is able to get, is slave of his habits. Slavery of habits and prejudices is of the worst type . . . Man is his own enemy; he can become his good friend also. We can have freedom or we can become our own slaves. It is all in our hands. This freedom is possible only through simple and pious life.

(Harijan Sevak; 10.19.1940)

When we talk about simplicity we often think of only simplicity in life style. Increasing our needs to live more comfortably and lavishly has several personal and social disadvantages. If many in the world find it difficult to have two meals in a day then it is not justified that some live lavishly. One would find it difficult to establish that it could be possible without inequitable distribution of wealth.

It is violent also, in the sense that those who are poor feel hurt when they find some others living in luxury. It generates negative emotions like envy and greed in the poor. Cruel display of wealth becomes the major cause of crime in any society.

One who is accustomed of luxurious life is deprived of many beautiful things and moments that can be enjoyed only when one lives as a humble partner of the wealthiest entity of the universe, the nature. Nothing can match the sight, the music, the touch, the smell and the taste Mother Nature can offer.

There is simplicity of thought; peacefully active, creative and sublime; that is; *satyam, shivam and sundaram*. Simplicity is not a product of our limited intellect but that of the divine.

There is also simplicity of speech without any superficial decoration of words that distract. Simple speech is the one where the words do not ride on the meaning but the meaning rides on the words. That is why it is heard not through ears but heart.

I cannot help thinking that it would be a great catastrophe, a great National tragedy, if you were to barter away your simplicity for this tinsel splendour.

(Mahatma; D.G. Tendulkar)

It is untruth that needs to be ostensibly decorated. Truth needs no cover-up. Truth is simple. When we are close to truth we start approaching simplicity in our thoughts, speech, lifestyle, behaviour and conduct. Gandhi was simplicity personified. I shall not be exaggerating if I say that one should feel Gandhi to understand him and to understand what simplicity is.

Do not be lifted off your feet; do not be drawn away from the simplicity of your ancestors.

(Mahatma; D.G. Tendulkar)

I am about to complete what I planned to discuss with my readers about the qualities a true **sadhak** must possess to achieve his goal (**sadhya**). We may recall that according to Gandhi **sadhya** was **truth** (because that was the only way to realize God), the tool (**sadhan**) was **non-violence** and **sadhak** were the operators; that is, all those who had taken upon them the task of realizing the truth. Gandhi saw truth in selfless service of humanity as that was serving the creation of God. I did not use the expression of 'training the operators (**sadhak**)'; instead I considered it as 'learning by **sadhak** through experiencing and experimenting'. This concept of Gandhi (although he never put it in so many words as I have dared to do relying on my own understanding of Gandhi) becomes abundantly clarified even in this chapter; when we find that simplicity cannot be learned or acquired; it is just like a by-product of one's approaching close to truth.

I would not claim that the list of qualities is exhaustive. During the course of his working, speaking in public or otherwise and writing; Gandhi referred to many qualities that he found surfacing before him on the vast sea of thoughts he was engulfed in. The vast sea of thoughts that Gandhi was engulfed in coexisted with his tireless actions, both empowering each other.

> *There is absolutely nothing like Gandhism in my mind. I am not an initiator of any sect. I have never claimed to be a 'tatva-gyani' (knower of truth). I am not working on any of these lines. People asked me to write about my thoughts . . . . If any of such things have to happen that may happen after my death. I have no such plans. I have simply thought and made efforts to actualize them, without any plan or scheme; on individual basis; to experiment extensively with eternal knowledge on issues like truth and non-violence in my daily life. Just like*

a child I got inspired and kept on doing whatever came before me in a flow.

(Gandhi Seva Sangh; Savali, 03.03.1936)

The things that appear to me to be good for the mankind I never forget them.

(The Diary of Mahadev Desai; Editor, N.D. Parikh)

The fact is that big things do not appear to me as actually big but small things become very big for me.

(The Diary of Mahadev Desai; Editor, N.D. Parikh)

It will be wrong to call me Sanyasi. The ideals I follow are worth adopting for the entire humanity. I have gained through them gradually, with my growth in life. I have received them step by step after deep contemplation. Celibacy and non-violence, I have adopted through my personal experience. They were essential for me to carry out my duties for the people.

. . . . all men and women can do what I have done. The only condition is that one should also make efforts with positive hope and shraddha. Action without shraddha makes one fall.

(Harijan Sevak; 10.03.1936)

God makes me write what I write. When I say this, it is literally true. When I read my own article in 'Young India', I feel I cannot write them again even if I want to. . . . For anything to happen there has to be a background.

(The Diary of Mahadev Desai; Editor, N.D. Parikh)

Gandhi was working and was always thinking about his work. In this process he spoke to others and wrote for others with a view to sharing his thoughts and findings with others. I have simply tried to pick up some of it according to my understanding.

Self-discipline is not an unshakable resolve like non-violence that demands **shraddha** or development of intuitive power to succeed. However, it is essential for any kind of learning. Let us say it is **rajas penance**.

The one who has resolved to adopt Dharma of selfless service should also resolve to remain poor. It means he should not take up any occupation or business that makes him shy of serving others.

(Satyagraha in South Africa; M.K. Gandhi)

I have reached to a conclusion that the gifts received by the one who is in service of the people, can never be treated as owned by him.

(My Experiments with Truth; M.K. Gandhi)

When we refuse to listen to the one opposed to us or make fun of him; we actually close our minds . . . . Although we have limited intelligence still it is our duty to courageously move ahead according to what our conscience says. However, we must keep our mind open and must always be prepared to accept if we are proved wrong.

(Harijan Sevak; 05.31.1942)

It is best if untruth is not responded to. Falsehood does not have any strength of its own. It dies its own death. If we oppose it, it may proliferate and circulate.

(Harijan Sevak; 06.22.1940)

Maintaining accounts has no relation with having confidence or having doubts. It, in itself is Dharma (duty).

(Satyagraha in South Africa; M.K. Gandhi)

I believe that the personal and public life of one who serves people must be well synchronized. . . . In my opinion it is wrong to think that good work ends if the one who did it is gone. I believe that truthful and solid work makes the worker immortal.

(Harijan Sevak; 03.02.1947)

A few sweet and pleasing words of appreciation can achieve what money **cannot** *achieve.*

(Satyagraha in South Africa; M.K.Gandhi)

The expression 'if possible' is like a poison for a firm resolve for actions meant for welfare of the others.

(Mangal Prabhat; Yarvada Jail, 10.14.1930)

One must use the things that he considers as his own in a manner that no harm is caused to others. This is a principle of equality. It is also a beautiful principle of moral conduct.

(Harijan Sevak; 09.21.1947)

One who works systematically and in an organized way never gets tired. It is never the excessive work that tires one; it is always the lack of systems and mismanagement of affairs that is tiring.

(Harijan Sevak; 06.16.1946)

Unless and until it is proved that one has not kept his words or that he had been telling lies; doubting him is not a dignified response.

(Harijan Sevak; 05.26.1946)

Hereinabove, I quoted a very few words of Gandhi that lay great emphasis on necessity of formulating a code of conduct for oneself and then sticking to it.

20

SECOND SHORT PAUSE

Sarve cha sukhinah **santu sarve santu niramayah,
Sarve bhadrani pashyantu ma kashchiddukhbhag
bhavet.**

[All should be happy, contended and be able to see
what is good for all. All should be healthy and no one
should suffer.]

This is a prayer to God from ancient Indian scriptures.

Having discussed the truth, the God and the tool to realize
both according to Gandhi, let us try to know what changes
Gandhi wanted to bring about in his surroundings.

There is no doubt that Gandhi's surroundings were
included in the universe or perhaps it is more appropriate
to say that the entire universe surrounded him. There is
no doubt that welfare of all was his only dream. Gandhi
thought about and worked for converting what might be
considered as ideal into reality. He not only said it in no
unclear words but also made sincere efforts to march ahead
in this direction throughout his life.

The first man on this earth, let us call him Adam, had no
problem in changing his surroundings. Had he walked

through five miles he could have found him in new surroundings. Perhaps, Adam could have found cleaner water, more fruit trees, better cave for protecting him and so on. As for Mr. Adam of today, he cannot change things so easily. He has a family, a society, a big chain of administrative machinery overseeing him, a few hundreds of laws and acts that bind him, his religious beliefs, his livelihood and numerous constrains that he has to worry about.

Take any problem or any issue; it needs to be defined as to what kind of problem or issue it is; a family one, a political one, a social one, an educational one, a religious one, an issue related to livelihood, or concerning one's individual freedom, a national one or a Global one; it is difficult to complete the list.

Let us get to the root of it. If we think about some change and decide to implement it, will we be able to do it? One of the simple answers could be, "If the change relates to our surroundings the task may not be simple." In some cases it can be so difficult that we cannot even imagine how the change would ever take place. For example if we want that ratio of earnings of the richest and the poorest in this world be made not to exceed 50:1 within 10 years; can we get it done? Irony of the situation is that perhaps 80% of the world's population would welcome this change but they would individually report that the change being thought of is impossible to achieve. For the sake of simplicity let us make the canvass much smaller. Can we train 40 postgraduate students from any of the universities in India or the U.S.A. from any discipline, within six months that they never speak a lie for the rest of their lives? The changes I proposed above are good from humanitarian point of view and a big majority of the world is expected to support them, still we find them a little strange. Gandhi thought that there was nothing strange about these tasks and we must attempt them wholeheartedly.

I have been a fighter since birth and have revolted against the system throughout my life.

(Harijan Sevak; 07.27.1947)

Man is indivisible. He cannot be divided into many categories, such as social, economical, political, religious etc. I do not recognize any Dharma (duty) other than welfare of human beings. All other things have no moral foundation; they are meaningless, cacophonous and farcical.

(Harijan Sevak; 01.07.1939)

Some say that I am the greatest revolutionary of my time. It may not be true. But I do consider myself as a revolutionary; a non-violent revolutionary.

(Mahatma Gandhi in England; Mahadev Desai)

We have seen in previous chapters that Gandhi's insistence for non-violence was total. He also made it clear from time to time that considerable amount of working on oneself was needed if one was determined to adopt the path of non-violence. Although Gandhi gave little credit to him or his own efforts for developing himself into a true **sadhak**; but through his autobiography and other writings it can be easily found that his revolution included revolting against himself, whom he always called an ordinary person. He often said, "If I could do it, others can also easily do it."

> *I have made assiduous efforts for half of a century so that I can clearly listen to my inner voice.*

(The Diary of Mahadev Desai; Editor, N.D.Parikh)

Next few chapters of this book are devoted to a few areas Gandhi identified where changes were necessary. He also discussed about the ways such changes could be brought about. This is being done to draw clear pictures of the ideals that needed to be converted into realities on priority basis according to Gandhi. This time the field of his experiments is primarily going to be India. No doubt, Gandhi worked for India after returning from South Africa and he was highly concerned about India but he always had in mind that success of his experiments with truth in India or elsewhere would show a path to the entire world, that is, the entire humanity. Restricting Gandhi according to his nationalistic feelings and commitments is an error that should not be made.

It is difficult to form a view about his thinking process. A true experimenter experiments to know; then he again experiments to confirm whether the findings of the preceding experiments were right. A child also does it. I think Gandhi was no different except that he was a man possessed by the thought of welfare of humanity. Next few chapters shall cover human society, reforms, the right livelihood, democracy, economic justice, social justice, caste and class struggles, co-operation, machines and physical labour, education, religions, women, importance of scriptures and other related fields.

21

OUR UNIVERSE

If we ask someone to name the place where he lives, he would tell some address in France, United States of America, Bermuda or any other nation in the world. He would not be wrong in the sense that in his present life his body is generally found at that address at the time the question was raised. We can neither ask a man where his mind lives nor would he be able to answer this question. Our Bermuda friend might have been thinking of England when we asked him about the address of his mind, but the moment the question is raised, his mind would leave England.

Things become more perplexing if we decide to give more importance to our souls than bodies. Gandhi writes;

> *The ultimate meaning of domicile* (used in the sense of *swadesh*, one's own country) *of our soul is freedom from all worldly relations. Even one's body is foreign to a soul, as it obstructs the soul from establishing relations and becoming united with other souls in the universe.*

**(Mangal Prabhat;
M.K.Gandhi, Navjeevan Trust)**

Gandhi completely dissolved the concept of universality into that of **Swadwshi**. **Swadeshi** means relating to one's own country. Man has limitations. If he wants to selflessly serve humanity, he individually, cannot think of serving the entire population of the world. That is not physically possible. The moment one relinquishes his selfishness and think of others; he takes the first step towards surrendering his self to universal consciousness. Gandhi said;

> . . . *Dedicating oneself completely for the service of one's immediate surroundings is Swadeshi Dharma. If one serves his immediate surrounding; people from distant lands are also served automatically. As against this if one is tempted to serve people from faraway places he is not able to serve them properly; and in the process he is also deprived of opportunity to serve his immediate surroundings.*

> *There is no selfishness in Swadwshi. In fact there is an opportunity for complete devotion to selfless service. If there is any selfishness in it, it is of very pure kind. One can become totally devoted to the cause of others' welfare.*

**(Mangal Prabhat;
M.K. Gandhi, Navjeevan Trust)**

What Gandhi is saying is poles apart from saying, 'Charity begins at home.' When one says, "Charity begins at home," the emphasis is on 'home' but when Gandhi says, "Serve Swadesh," emphasis is on 'selfless service'.

Gandhi had only self-less service of humanity in mind. And this service was to be done by human beings. The one who serves derives spiritual benefit and the one who is served derives primarily materialistic benefit. Spiritual benefit is derived if one gets detached from greed, avarice, fear, malice, pride, hatred, excessive attachment toward things that are short-lived and destructible, cruelty anger etc.; and develops good qualities like divine love, selflessness, forgiveness, patience, mercy, devotion to God, benevolence, concern and care for those who are in pain, weak, poor or needy and many other such qualities. Those who need to be served are those who are in pain and sorrow caused due to physical disabilities, damages or diseases; act of God or torments of nature; unjust treatment, oppression or violence of any kind by man, animals etc. (that is due to *daihik, daivik* or *bhautik reasons*). Those who are to be served have to be in real need of service. One who serves must have sufficient knowledge about the root causes of the problems, nature of problems and how to enable and empower those who need service; so that they can be made competent to best possible extent to deal with their problems. For this it is necessary that the one who serves understands abilities, disabilities, aspirations, preferences, prejudices and limitations of those that are to be served. If the one who needed to be served is served well, the service by itself becomes an example for others to follow.

This may be clarified by way of an example. If some selfless village youth, from a poverty stricken village, devoid of facilities of basic education and any employment opportunities; pledge to serve their own village; and with right efforts succeed in making their village happy and vibrant with life; with every child receiving basic education and each adult having enough employment; the effort of those village youth may become an example and source of inspiration for many other villages. That is what Gandhi meant in this context when he said, *"If one serves his immediate surrounding; people of distant lands are also served automatically."* Gandhi said;

> *If one is able to convert a single village into an ideal village, it means he has discovered a way for the entire world. A sadhak should not be tempted to do things that cannot be properly done.*

(Harijan Sevak; 08.03.1940)

> *One should avoid doing what is beyond his capability and capacity. Further, one should also not be satisfied by doing things which are below his ability and capacity.*

One who succeeds doing things beyond his ability becomes victim of pride and worldly attachments and the one who does less than his ability is a thief.

(The Diary of Mahadev Desai; Edited by N.D. Parikh)

It has become very important to quote from Geeta at this stage. I have repeatedly said that Geeta appears to be one of the main sources of Gandhi's inspiration. In fact, he himself has admitted it at several occasions. Hence, my readers should not give any credit to me for this initiative.

**Karmanaiva hi sansiddhim aasthitah Jankadayah,
Lokasangraham aiva api sampashyan kartum arhasi.**

(Geeta; Chapter III, shloka 20)

[Translation: Great people, like King Janak could achieve what is worth achieving (*siddhi*) through *Karmayoga*. Therefore, looking at appropriate human conduct (*lokasangrha*); you should also act selflessly.

Meaning: *Karma-yoga* has been interpreted by scholars as actions or acts without desire for the fruits of the action. Gandhi treated it as selfless service. Geeta says that Great King Janak (It is believed that Janak was a king who was considered a *Rishi* because of his knowledge and conduct) achieved *siddhi* (exalted position) due to his selfless deeds. Geeta advices that one must follow king Janak's example; and in view of such deeds being in the nature of *lokasangraha*; one must do all his deeds affecting the external world selflessly. Scholars have explained that any action must be according to place (country) one lives in, the time he is living in and the circumstances existing at the time of his life; it should be consistent with the conduct prescribed by scriptures to benefit all and should not be directed to satisfy his desires for worldly personal gains; in a nutshell that work or action must become an example of right action and right conduct for universal good, for others to follow.]

22

OUR FREEDOM

❧⚖❧

*If as a member of a slave nation I could
deliver the suppressed classes from their
slavery without freeing myself from my
own, I would do so today. But it is an
impossible task. A slave has not the
freedom even to do the right thing.*

(Mahatma; D.G. Tendulkar)

To understand true meaning of the above quotation of
Gandhi it is of paramount importance that we understand
the meaning of the word 'free'. Sanskrit word for 'free' is
swatantra. It is composed of two words; **swa** and **tantra**;
swa means *my, mine* or *our*; **tantra** means, a system
of laws or rules that binds one who is in that system.
Therefore, **swatantra** means one who, through his own
free will binds himself with certain laws and rules. The
word **swatantra** has no sense of complete or absolute
freedom or some kind of anarchy; it has a sense of binding
oneself, not with the laws framed by others or external
laws enforced externally. **Swatantra** means remaining
under the control of oneself. Just as freedom is a noun
formed with the word free, **Swatantrata** is a noun formed
with the word **swatantra**.

According to ancient Indian philosophy the entire creation of the God is bound by divine laws. All that is animate or inanimate, is actually ruled and controlled by the Supreme power (the God); but the animate like human being in its physical existence, erroneously, binds itself or becomes captive of its own physical existence and considers things that are actually not its own, as its own. One who becomes detached to worldly affairs does not remain captive; he becomes free or **swatantra**. It does not mean that he becomes free of divine laws. In fact, as divinity is our true nature. We come under control of our true nature only when we relinquish our subordination to what is not divine. Many *Rishis* in ancient India were believed to be free from all kinds of captivities. Why India alone, we know in the entire world there had always been people who were 'free' even under the most tyrannical rules. Was Gandhi a slave when British ruled India? No, he was not. Did Gandhi believe that India had become free when British left India on 15th August, 1947? No, he did not.

> *Freedom means maintaining our control on ourselves. This can be done only by those who have righteous conduct, follow right policies, harm no one, deceive no one and honour their duties towards their mothers, fathers, wives, children, servants, neighbours etc. Such people would always be free whichever country they may be living in. The nation where such people are*

in majority may be considered as a nation that is free.

**(Sarvodaya;
Edited by Vinoba Bhave and others)**

In the language of religion Ramarajya means rule of God on the earth. If translated in the language of politics it would mean; a democracy where poor-rich, women-men, whites and blacks etc. live happily; and all inequalities and discrimination do not exist for people of different castes, creeds and religion. In such rule, ownership of all the land and power to rule would be with the people. Such political system shall be constituted on the foundation of truth and non-violence. Such political system shall be distinguishable through its happy, prosperous and self-dependent villages and the village people.

(Panchagani, 06.06.1945)

In this chapter we have come to a stage from where we have to seek answers to many questions. A few of such questions are as under. What is real freedom in worldly sense? Is it right if a nation where the ruler or the Government is concerned about its people and its laws are based on justice to all, think of acquiring control of some other nation; where people are suffering due to misrule existing there; with a view to providing justice to the people of latter nation? Is democracy the best system and what is true democracy? Is freedom something that can be granted or is it right if a nation supports the people of other nation to obtain its freedom? If and why all efforts for obtaining freedom must be founded on truth and non-violence? Can a nation become a nation of slaves even if it is ruled by its own people? What is the intent of Gandhi when he emphasizes on existence of self-dependent villages? There can be many more questions but in my opinion the above questions would sufficiently clarify many issues that have existed in past, exist today or may exist in future.

Answers of many questions shall emerge in subsequent chapters but a few of the important thoughts of Gandhi can be discussed in this chapter itself. Gandhi said;

> *The freedom that is achieved with the efforts of others, howsoever, kind and well-meaning, they may be, cannot be sustained for long; as the external help and support cannot be expected to last forever. Such freedom is not true freedom. But when, even the most fallen and downtrodden of the people learn the art of achieving their freedom through non-violent non-cooperation with the unwanted rulers; those in captivity cannot*

avoid experiencing the light freedom spreads.

(Harijan Sevak; 04.20.1940)

Learning the art of achieving freedom; it has two objectives involved in it. First is preparing oneself for being free and second is making the one who rules over others against their will, realize his mistake. The first is more important. Why? To understand, let us take up an example. When we remove the one (say, an unwanted ruler) who may be ruling over us against our will; we create a void that has got to be filled in to regulate our worldly life in many ways. There is nothing wrong if we assume that we are a selfish, violent and greedy people. Then there is a strong possibility that, after getting rid of the unwanted rulers, those who are greedier, more violent and more powerful amongst us would become freer to harm those who are weak. Perhaps the unwanted ruler whom we have removed was able to exercise enough control over such selfish and violent people (maybe in his personal interests and without good intentions), that made the lives of the weak relatively safe. Let me clarify this with a real-life example. I distinctly remember, from my childhood days, many comments from my elders that implied that British Raj was more efficient and just in many respects than the rule of free India. It is highly relevant to quote Gandhi again;

When independence arrives after dependence, all social evils come up on

*the surface. Instead of being disturbed
about it we must keep our mind steady to
solve problems.*

(Harijan Sevak; 06.01.1947)

The basic thought that is emerging from the discussions
so far is that freedom is not that much about getting rid
of the external undesired influences but it is more about
empowering the right existing within us. Empowering the
right within us has two connotations. The first has to deal
with our worldly existence and the second is about our
spiritual growth. The word that was often used in place of
swatantrata was **swarajya**. As already said **swa** means
my, mine, our etc. and **rajya** means *rule.* For survival of
the universe, in general and for the humanity, in particular;
rules and laws are essential. Both cannot be allowed to be
absolutely free or independent. When we say **swarajya**
we mean self-rule in worldly sense and when we say
swatantrata we mean self-rule in a sense that is slightly
more biased towards the laws of the divine.

While we are in this discussion we cannot afford to
forget that even our worldly existence along with all
happiness and pains associated therewith; becomes much
less painful, if it is well controlled and regulated by our
spiritual existence. Gandhi said;

*God's voice is expressed through the deeds
of man.*

(Harijan Sevak; 12.30.1939)

Therefore, we can confidently say that our struggle for independence begins from the day we initiate action to empower the right within us. When we start approaching close to practical or immediate truth a process begins within us to make us aware of the path that is to be followed by us. The path that leads to the right approach and conduct to be adopted by us to deal with those who are hindrance in our way to freedom and the path that leads to our appropriate spiritual growth to help us conduct in a right manner when we physically achieve freedom. That appropriate *spiritual growth*, we have just referred to is to help us internalize the laws of the divine, our true nature, the **swa** of **swatantrata** and **swarajya**. If we start thinking of the word independence instead of freedom; to understand the curse of dependence; and start calling it self-dependence (instead of independence) we will be reaching close to Gandhi's views. But when we start contemplating about **self** as *spirit, soul* or *Atma*; the part of *Paramatma* (the God); that is, our true nature, and the divine laws that define and decide our true nature we would have fully understood the theory and practice of Gandhi's concept of **swatantrata.**

By listening to our inner voice how do we prepare ourselves for self-rule; that is, how we regulate our conduct through our own efforts; to live happily in our worldly life, knowing full well that unless appropriate spiritual guidance is not forthcoming from within us, we cannot be happy even in our worldly life? Can we afford to be violent with ourselves in any way i.e. physically, mentally or vocally? I am confident of receiving a unanimous reply saying, "NO". Well, if that is what we are learning to prepare ourselves for our impending freedom (of course, that cannot be without our assiduous efforts), how is it possible that we would involve ourselves in violence during our struggle for freedom?

So, that was about the first part (preparing ourselves for **swatantrata**) of *learning the art of achieving freedom* that we considered to be more important. Now we shall move on to the second part.

Is it possible to make a nation who rules over other nation against the latter's wishes realize its mistake?

> *In a violent war anger towards the enemy goes on increasing day by day. In the dictionary of non-violence there, as such, is no external enemy; however, even if some enmity is assumed to exist; non-violence requires that feeling of kindness and love must be developed against the enemy. One who is non-violent knows that no one is evil by choice. Everybody has a capacity to differentiate between virtues and vice. Non-violence has the power to enhance the quality of righteousness in one whose actions are not just.*

(Harijan Sevak; 10.12.1940)

In modern times no one would discard non-violence altogether just because it is a new concept. Also, no one would call it impossible just because it is difficult to apply. The world has seen things that have become old and new things that looked impossible in past. I am convinced that there is much more than eyes can see in non-violence. The history of various religions is replete with such instances.

(Harijan Sevak; 08.24.1940)

In modern times we do not generally have individuals ruling over countries. Either the rule is of elected representatives or of political parties or some other kinds of assemblies. Further, people of different countries do have at least some say in the affairs of the Governments. In such circumstances it is impossible to believe that non-violence would have no supporters in a particular country, especially when man, as always in past, by and large is still religious. We all know that, without exception all religions preach non-violence. The very fact the democracies have replaced dictatorial regimes in most parts of the world, goes in to prove that the man essentially is in favour of non-violence. Perhaps it is impractical to expect that some country that have been ruling over another country would, at the end of its rule over the country; would make a public announcement about the mistake it committed of having kept the other country in captivity. But it is also true that the closeness between the citizens of the two countries (the ruler and the ruled) would increase if the struggle for freedom by the captive country remained non-violent throughout. The necessary condition for building honourable relations between the ruler and the ruled; after the end of the unjust rule of the unwanted ruler; is that all the three types of non-violence (physical, mental and oral) is strictly adhered to during the freedom struggle by the ruled country. Once healthy relations are developed between the citizens of the two countries; is there a need of thinking about realization of mistakes by the ruler country? I think it serves no other purpose for the country that was ruled except that it should not do the same thing to any other country as that was done to it. The ruled country should avoid getting influenced by those factors that prompted the ruler country get involved with violence.

The country that had been an oppressor must, however, identify the root causes that made it an oppressor in past and must try to eliminate them. The ruler country must come closer to the non-violent country that it ruled, to learn the factors and qualities that made it non-violent.

Causing harm of any type to a nation by another nation in self interest is violence. The present world is not free from this. Unfortunately, the leaders who do it are considered successful leaders. The right spiritual thought is that the one, who rises with violent means, ultimately falls.

Gandhi's thoughts provide the right path to those who are oppressed, "Do not accept violence meekly. Resist till the problem is solved. But, remember to protest and resist non-violently." A true non-violent resistance is the right solution for all those who may be suffering due to violence of others.

Gandhi said;

> *Total swarajya (self-rule) means not depending on the kindness of any other country. To prove this India has a big army of people ready to even sacrifice their lives, if that becomes necessary. But we will not kill others, come what may . . . . Many think that freedom can be achieved through violence. It shall be a very unfortunate day for India if it achieves freedom going over the pools of blood.*
>
> *If India gets its freedom after taking up arms then the day of establishing world peace in true sense will get postponed indefinitely. World history has been a history of wars; we are trying to write a new history.*

(Harijan Sevak; 07.10.1937)

The next question that can be answered in this chapter itself is; whether a nation that is concerned about its people and holds justice in high esteem should come forward for rescuing people of some other nation if they are suffering due to misrule in their own country? In the immediately preceding quotation Gandhi does not agree.

Gandhi's thoughts have two very important elements, apart from many others. First is about 'serving the people selflessly' and the second is, 'fighting any injustice non-violently'. In the last chapter we came to be aware of his concept of 'serving immediate surroundings only'. It is evident that, making the world a place worth living was in Gandhi's mind. If a nation decides to serve the people of some other country it would make that country dependent on it. The laws of truth and non-violence demand that each one of us is required to fight any injustice non-violently. If one allows someone else to fight his battle he loses an opportunity to learn what he must learn for performing his Dharma (duty) and living his life in a way that helps in making spiritual as well as necessary materialistic advancements. Further, true freedom (**swarajya**) can be achieved only when people learn to achieve it for their benefit and for the benefit of their future generations. The nation that helps the suffering nation cannot provide that much as can be achieved with self efforts by the suffering nation. More over the helping nation may, in this process, cause neglect to its own people. However, any nation can create or develop some knowledge for the benefit of humanity without expecting anything in return. For example, Gandhi developed valuable knowledge for the welfare of the world and passed it on to all who care to use it.

God demands nothing less than complete self-surrender as the price for the only real freedom that is worth having.

(Truth is God; Editor, R.K. Prabhu)

23

DEMOCRACY

Democracy comes naturally to him who is habituated normally to yield willing obedience to all laws, human or divine.

(Mahatma; D.G.Tendulkar)

That nation, where majority of people are able to manage their personal affairs in a sufficiently organized manner without any external control; can be called a democratic nation in real sense. Where such conditions do not exist democracy does not exist. This can be proved.

(Harijan Sevak; 11.09.1935)

As long as a democracy is based on violence it cannot protect the weak and the poor. We know that there is no place for the weak in countries ruled by dictators. According to my understanding there should be equal opportunity for people at the top of the hierarchy as well as those

at the bottom in a democratic system. But,
this is not possible without non-violence.

(Harijan Sevak; 05.18.1940)

From the above quotations we find that Gandhi gave importance to the following two factors for a democratic system.

Firstly, there should be minimum possible control from those who rule; but the lack of control should not result into situations whereby the people face problems in performing their own work. When majority of people conduct themselves appropriately so as not to harm others, necessity of controls is minimized. However, if the rulers in a democracy of people having good character and appropriate conduct still exercise control, it may indicate that either the rulers rule in their own self interests or they do not know how to rule. This situation can arise if and when the people make mistakes in electing their representatives.

Secondly, there should be equal opportunities for growth and development for all irrespective of his economic, social or cultural status. In practice, this stipulation is not that fair as it appears on the face of it. There is a great difference between individuals due to variety of reasons. All cannot derive fairly uniform benefit from the opportunities available to them. Gandhi was very well aware of this. I will not hesitate in saying that he was more aware of this problem than most of philosophers, politicians and thinkers of his time; and I wish to add that even after him no one has ever reached to those depths of the problems to which Gandhi could reach. It is not that Gandhi was superior to all others in any manner. Gandhi could reach deeper than others simply because he cared to feel, to experience and to experiment. This needs to be elaborated.

Each society, each nation and each individual; apart from all other factors; is a product of history. Very rarely, in our history of about last one thousand years or so (the part we are better aware of) Man had been fair to his fellow human being. The expression 'very rarely' simply implies that good, howsoever small, has always existed and still exists. Perhaps, this had been a period when man; in an ecstasy of playing with the new toys he had explored and was continuously exploring with his newly acquired capabilities; carelessly discarded the wisdom his ancestors had acquired by experiencing life and experimenting with it. This wisdom was to always keep the man at the centre of everything.

No doubt, man learned many new things. But, much fascinated by his 'continuously increasing achievements,' he defaulted more and more. While man defaulted more, he gave little importance to unloading of some loads from the bundle of his 'sins' that was proliferating. These 'sins' accrued because man neglected or used fellow human beings in his personal interests. Man's desire to use whatever is material (that includes fellow human beings) to please his senses are insatiable. Man thinks that he can solve his problems with some methods that he can device, some technologies he can develop, some 'cracies' he can think of and some 'isms' that he can follow. He does not realize that he has limitations. His intellect also suffers from serious limitations.

When Gandhi waged a war against all kind of discriminations like discriminations according to castes, religions, gender, colour of skin, cultures, class, sects, intellectual labour and physical labour etc; he targeted at 'the bundle of past sins as well as newly added sins of man'. Whenever Gandhi spoke about democracy, the history of man's sins must have been crossing his mind. That is why he was invariably found referring to them whenever the issue of equality and equity came before him.

I reproduce below a portion of the last quotation from Gandhi for the convenience of my readers in this context.

> *According to my understanding there should be equal opportunity for people at the top of the hierarchy as well as those at the bottom in a democratic system. But, this is not possible without non-violence.*

When Gandhi says that equality is not possible without non-violence he expresses a great concern for man's **vritti** (related to duties, actions and sensory involvements for survival in the external world) of discriminating. Discrimination is not inert. When we differentiate for convenience of identification it is fine. For example, when a mother ties a black thread around the neck of one of the exactly identical newly born twins to avoid a situation when one is not fed and the other is fed twice or thrice; it is not discrimination. But, when a low caste devotee is disallowed to enter a temple it is discrimination. When, according to democratic principle you legally allow him to enter the temple but the other high caste devotees inside the temple maintain some distance from him, it means discrimination still exists.

The low caste devotee feels hurt. Therefore it is violence. Man is carrying the load of violence that he caused for years and years. He is not doing anything about that load, instead he is continuing with fresh violence because of his greed and hatred; that is why he is restless. Man wants love but he does not love anybody, not even himself. Man wants peace, but acts only to disturb peace. Man does not want to be harmed but he does not know that most of his actions and activities done in a day have caused harm to someone, somewhere.

> *For sustaining democracy people need to live with and stick to the feeling of freedom (swa+tantra+ta), self-pride and oneness. They have to possess the vritti of electing truthful people to represent them.*

(My Experiments with Truth; M.K. Gandhi)

Here I have quoted Gandhi using Sanskrit word for freedom in parentheses. I find this quote very meaningful to understand what true democracy could be. A participant in democracy must conduct himself in his worldly life according to divine laws. That makes him **swatantra** (free). He is self-controlled, needing no one to control him. Self-pride helps him to feel ashamed when he falters in his conduct. His shame prompts him to rectify his errors and also to make good the loss caused by his poor conduct. I have used the word *oneness* instead of *unity.* Gandhi had faith in **advait. Advait** means 'not two'; that is, only one. In ancient Indian scriptures there are two concepts to express relation between God and the nature. When we say that *jeevatma* (we, along with what is animate in nature) and what is inanimate in nature are separate from the God; it is **dvait** (two). No doubt, the God governs us and we are totally dependent on Him, still we are two different entities; that is **dvait. Dvait** accepts existence of two separate entities.

As against this when we say that God is one, an infinite one; that divides Itself into infinite parts and still remains one, the infinite one; we speak of 'no two' but one, or **advait**. Gandhi always spoke about realizing God. He treated a poor farmer or one from very low caste belonging to the same One Whole to whom we all belong; that is, we all including the God belong to the same ONE INFINITE WHOLE. He said;

> *We want to prove advait with thirty crores*
> *of people. That can happen only when*

we become like zero. Politics of power is falsehood. We have to do what others look down upon; such constructive work we shall do.

**(Gandhi Seva Sangh;
Malikanda, 02.22.1940)**

So, that *oneness (advait)* Gandhi referred to in the quote (immediately preceding the last one) we were discussing. We often find a group of good people elect someone who is not as good as they desire him to be. It happens because we do not often apply the right considerations for electing our representatives. We may bias our opinions with issues like education, caste, religion, gender, status in society etc. and may give least importance to the main issue, that is; candidates' dedication to serve the people selflessly. People should not have tendency to discriminate a man from another man on worldly considerations.

There is existence of only **one**, the existence of **the Supreme**, the universal existence we may call it. We are infinite parts of it. When we realize that we individually are a very insignificant part we become aware of our extreme smallness. We become like zero. But at the same time, when we realize that in spite of being a very insignificant part we also have a role to play in the affairs of the universe we become 'very important participants' in the affairs of the universe. We must realize that our individual actions, thoughts and conduct affect the universe. Therefore, we, individually, are responsible for the affairs of the world and hence, have duties to perform. If we do not perform our duties properly, the universe would be adversely affected and as consequences thereof we shall also suffer. This is the essence of **praja** (people) + **tantra** (a system of laws). In Sanskrit we use **prajatantra** for democracy. If we understand this, we understand what Gandhi had in mind for democracy.

> *In my view to rule cannot be our aim. Of all sadhan (tools) that empower the people to grow in all the departments of life; political power is also one. Political power is the power that helps representatives of the people to guide and regulate lives of people as a nation. If national life could become so perfect so as to make any guidance and regulations redundant, the representatives of the people also become redundant. That could be considered as a system of civilized and cultured anarchy.*

> *In this kind of system each individual would be his own ruler. Each individual of such a nation will guide and regulate himself in a manner that no harm is caused to his neighbour. When in such ideal conditions there would not be any existence of a state, why would there be a need of political rule? That is why*

Thoreau has said, "That government is best which rules the least."

**(Sarvodaya;
Editors, Vinoba Bhave and others)**

If laws and rule become necessary to teach people what honesty is; it means democracy has developed cracks in it. Democracy lives and survives on faith.

(Harijan Sevak; 11.16.1947)

24

RIGHT LIVELIHOOD

No living being that exists at present or will ever exist in future can disassociate him from the thought of food. Even the greatest of devotees of God think of food if hunger grips them. In Hindi there is a phrase, '*papi pet*'. *Papi* means sinner and *pet* means stomach. In the strictest of spiritual or religious laws forgiveness is recommended for sins committed to save one's life. If I am pardoned for my daring attempt to speak like Gandhi, I would say, **"The first and foremost duty before us is to ensure that man does not become a cause of hunger for any human being, for all times to come."**

Have we, as ordinary human beings realized the above referred immediate truth (practical truth or *vyavaharik satya*)? If I am one of the 100 employees of a company that produces cloth for the entire population of the world; am I earning my livelihood in a right way? Please do not think that I have presented a situation that is impossible to actualize. We know that technological growth has perhaps achieved geometrical proportions in last few years. Advanced technologies have almost eliminated hand weaving, allied activities and cottage industries in cloth manufacturing sector. We need not accept any ill-conceived statistical answers to this question. We are aware of the predicament of many artisans, when many rural and cottage industries were phased out to make way for modern technologies. We can easily imagine what would have happened to the weavers who earned their livelihood by weaving till date and what may happen to those presently employed in textile manufacturing if only 100 people are needed to manufacture cloth for the entire world.

Being humanitarian means being concerned about those who are in difficulty and are in pain. I am well aware that if I present arguments against the ways world has advanced over last one and a half century; I will not be able to create even a small ripple in the sea of thoughts that prevail in the minds of about 20% of world population that has succeeded and is succeeding in forcing its plans and ideas on the entire world. I would further say that the figure of 20% may also be the very liberal; it could be even be as small as 5% for all one knows, for even the democracies that are rated as the best, represent their people only partially.

I will attempt, on the basis of my observations and understanding, to draw a comparison of what has occurred in my immediate surroundings over the last 45 years or so. There is no doubt that our material possessions have increased. Many of the possessions have contributed in giving us only psychological advantage in reducing our inconveniences of yesteryears. The gap between people has widened. Those much above the threshold of survival in 1970 went up, in terms of living conditions, noticeably and those below it also went up but only marginally or in rare cases, moderately. The majority of people in this world were struggling for their survival in 1970 and they continue to struggle even today. The level of contentment has dropped substantially in last fifty years in all age groups. Yet another thing that I have clearly noticed is that people, in general, have become more demonstrative, in the sense, that they present things associated with them as being better and bigger than what they actually are. I am refraining myself from saying that people have become less genuine but I suspect this may also occur if the present trend continues. If I am asked to write in a sentence the difference between 1970 and 2014, I would write; over the years goods and greed both have proliferated. No statistics, no expert remark from a renowned economist or a social scientist; it is a view from an ordinary adult individual.

I belong to India, a country having about 17.3% of world's population; with low per capita income but high in knowledge, whether modern or ancient; and hence, to quite some extent, representative of what is going on in the world. I am not convinced that we are moving on a path that ensures that man would not become a cause of hunger for any human being in all times to come. Like God, the principles of economics are also not detached from human beings. The human nature, **vrittis** of man are capable of throwing the best of statistically justified economic predictions off their balance. The situation becomes more critical when the physical world that has great influence on human being transforms human **vrittis** into strong prejudices. There are very strong reasons to suspect that human efforts to feed mankind have deviated from the path of truth.

> *Man must move according to how the God has made him with his hands and legs. He must realize his limits. If we do not travel; far and wide with high speed transport systems like trains etc.; we can save ourselves from many troubles. God has defined our limits by the bodies he gave us, but man has found ways to trespass those limits. Man was given intellect to explore God but he utilized it to win over the God. God made man to serve his immediate surroundings but he started running around to serve the entire universe. For serving the world one has to take help from people of different nature, culture and religions; he cannot bear this load and finally gives up.*

(Hind Swarajya; M.K. Gandhi)

The issue Gandhi discussed in the above quotation, on the face of it, does not appear to be closely linked to what we were discussing; but it is. Here Gandhi spoke about how to serve humanity efficiently and appropriately. Gandhi's initial lines are very meaningful. History tells us and we also clearly observe today, that it is basically human ego and greed that is making him go places, with superfast speed. Man does not fly from one corner of the world to another to serve humanity; he flies to secure more comfort, more luxury, more wealth, bigger status and higher prestige for himself. His entire attention is focused on how to give the best material outcome from all his efforts. He dedicated himself to the result of his work without bothering about the means he adopted. He focuses on achieving the greatest benefit for himself and the one for whom he works.

Not that the man is not aware of his folly but he glorifies his stupidity by convincing himself that he is doing some great job for the universe and that he is generating some great knowledge that had never existed in this world. Ironically, by working as aforesaid he becomes an example for the modern man as to how one must commit his life to earn his livelihood.

In this book, in earlier chapters we had been discussing about *Nishkam Karma*, i.e. action without any desire for its fruits. We talked about dedicating the fruits of action to the God; or as Gandhi viewed, to the creation of God, the humanity. Efforts of modern man for his livelihood are totally opposite of *Nishkam Karma*. Today when one earns his livelihood using his intellect that enables him to lead a life of luxury he dedicates the fruits of his action to himself and himself alone.

The argument that may be placed before us would be; that if some are able to use their superior intellect to satisfy human needs and are able to earn more to live more comfortably than others, what is wrong with it? I would say that there is nothing wrong in it provided reasonable needs of entire human population are satisfied first. Unfortunately, the economics of complete dependence on human intellect for satisfying reasonable needs for of the mankind upholding the principles of human dignity for centuries has not been evolved so far. This is a reality. This economy is based on creating more needs and satisfying them for a certain length of time leaving the reasonable needs of many always unsatisfied. This economy relies on generating more heart problems to sell pace makers that have been invented and manufactured. This is just like creating more conditions of war to create the need of advanced weapons just because someone has developed knowledge for producing advanced war weapons and someone else has made huge investments for producing weaponry based on that knowledge. Defective use of human intellect can create violence but cannot end it.

At this stage it is necessary to understand what is livelihood. When a man is born on this earth it is his Dharma (duty) to maintain his body-mind complex in top order so that he can properly serve the God or His creation. It is also his duty to take care of his family. He is also duty bound to arrange for appropriate education for his children so that they become capable of serving humanity selflessly. Organizing adequate resources or **sadhan** for performance of above referred duties is called earning one's livelihood. Earning anything more for his comfort or for the comfort of his family, earning for the purpose of providing for the future or storing for future or earning for satisfying one's sensory desires or inventing ways and means for satisfying insatiable human desires just for more pleasure and enjoyment; is not earning livelihood. If any one does it, it amounts to encroaching into the legitimate rights of others. In this context, the word legitimate does not refer to any laws framed by man; it is the right granted to all who are born on this earth so that there is enough for all to live on.

> *In my opinion the economy of India and that of the entire world must be such that no one is forced to live without food and clothes to cover them. In other words all must get enough to satisfy their basic necessities. This ideal can be achieved only if and when the people have undiluted rights on the sadhan (resources) that provide for satisfaction of basic necessities. Just as air and water are free for all, sadhan for satisfaction of basic necessities must also be available in adequate measures without interruption. These sadhan (resources) can never be allowed to become commodities for transactions that deprive anyone of his rights.*

(Sarvodaya; M.K. Gandhi)

The above statement of Gandhi does not imply that one who is born on this earth would get enough food and clothes even if he does not make necessary efforts for this. Gandhi insisted that each one of us must do physical labour for earning our livelihood. All religions are uncompromising about honesty. Marxism insists that those who do physical labour must get what is rightfully due to them. Gandhi says one can be honest only if he does physical labour for earning his livelihood. The above quote clears the 'field' where each one of us would physically work to earn our food and produce clothes to cover our bodies. He clears the field by insisting that the resources for generating food and clothes cannot be allowed to become commodities for transactions'. If I am permitted to put things bluntly, I would say that Gandhi meant that one who earns his livelihood without putting in physical (bodily) labour he is not honest.

I am aware that we are not accustomed to think on this issue on the lines Gandhi thought. I therefore request my readers to stay with the intent of Gandhi's thought on this issue and not to listen to the counter arguments that our mind generates, at least for some time. If we do this, we will perhaps be able to explore a new and useful knowledge that was not available to us. We all know that we must; first try to settle the right 'intent' in our minds; as only then we can arrive at the right 'content' that is beneficial for us. Right 'content' means wisdom that enables us to take right action.

> *Yajna could be of different types. One of them could be 'shram yajna'. If everybody earns his food only by doing physical labour, there cannot be any shortage of*

food and all would also have sufficient leisure.

Intellectual labour keeps our souls satisfied. It helps our atma (soul, spirit) achieve its right growth. Intellectual labour is satisfying of its own; there cannot be a need for earning any wages through it. . . . The society that exists on the laws of physical labour will give rise to a peaceful revolution. That revolution will make the social being free of drudgeries of 'struggle for life" and in its place; enjoyable process of competing for making gains through selfless service; will be established. The human society will then have human laws in place of laws of beasts.

(Harijan Sevak; 07.05.1935)

We have already discussed in this book that *yajna* primarily is concerned about human efforts for his physical existence. In the first paragraph of the above quotation Gandhi speaks about *shram-yajna. Shram* means physical labour. Here, Gandhi emphasizes that human effort for his physical existence must primarily be the efforts that he makes by using his body. In short, Gandhi says, *'Use your body for your physical existence and use your intellect for your spiritual existence'.*

*Doing physical labour for earning bread
is an economic principle that is based
on consciousness of life. It means every
human being must do physical labour to
earn food and clothes for him.*

(Harijan Sevak; 09.21.1947)

Geeta says;

**Aivam pravartitam chakram na anuvartayati iha
yaha;
Aghayuha indriyaramah mogham Parth sa
jeevati.**

(Geeta; Chapter III, shloka 16)

[Translation and Meaning: One who does not conduct
himself according to traditionally known and accepted
cycles of nature; spends his life remaining fully involved
with sensory pleasures; and thus living a lowly life full of
sins, wastes his life, without achieving anything from it.]

Gandhi said;

*Labour that is done for survival is yajna
according to Geeta. He who consumes
more than what is necessary for his own
survival; commits theft. As such people do
not work even that much as is needed. I
believe that no one is entitled to have more*

*than what is essential for his survival.
Even those who work hard are also not
entitled for more.*

*. . . Physical labour is always necessary
for producing things for human survival.
In whatever field necessary for human
needs man does physical labour; it
ultimately is bread labour.*

*It has been found that nature produces
enough for survival of all living beings. If
some draws more than what is necessary
for him, his neighbor has to go hungry.
The fact is that many in this world draw
many times more than their requirements.
The result is that many in world have to
remain unfed or underfed.*

**(Satyagraha Ashram Ka Itihas;
M.K. Gandhi)**

Although we have had discussions on the above lines
earlier in this book, let us discuss it again with some
examples in context of right livelihood. In past when
concept of democracy was not evolved, the kings and
his courtiers lived in luxury. They forced many from
their people to do physical labour to arrange things of
luxury for them; for example, they occupied big chunks
of land for constructing palaces, to make play grounds
for them or for producing such things that could not be

used to satisfy hunger. They forced many farmers to do such unproductive jobs that only satisfied the desires of rulers and their families. At times, farm activities were seriously hampered and there was little to eat for the people especially when nature also was not kind enough. Cruel and mindless actions of many kings for satisfaction of their sensory desires caused much harm to people. It is not difficult to understand that poverty was the side effect of violence.

Time changed, human intelligence helped man to enhance his capacities to produce more with less effort. No doubt, he discovered or invented because the God had granted him the desire to explore and intelligence to create. But despite this, the man could not help himself. Man thought that he was the master and could conquer the nature. Man surrendered to his *ahamkara,* his sensory desires and wavering mind. Those who possessed the intelligence to innovate failed to align their intelligence with universal intelligence. They did not serve God's creation, the nature and the humanity selflessly, instead they submitted to their desire to live more comfortably, to live life of luxury and get involved with sensory pleasures just like the rulers of the past. Such people were not large in numbers. There were also people who were powerful. Most of them were selfish and had violent nature. They were also not large in numbers. They had amassed wealth using violent means. The powerful and the intelligent joined hands. A new class came in existence that used its intelligence 'to generate large income for itself'. The natural resources that mankind traditionally used for his survival by putting in his physical efforts, were snatched away by this class. The intelligent ones used their innovations to produce more from such resources with marginal physical efforts. To back this 'new class' were the violent minds similar to those of the oppressive kings and feudal lords, the plunderers and invaders who moved around the world for snatching away the natural resources belonging to others through physical force or by cheating and there were also the minds of the intelligent ones who could invent or innovate to produce more with less physical efforts. It is difficult to say whether the powerful lured the intelligent ones in this game or the intelligent ones offered their services to the powerful. No doubt there had been cases where humanity was well served through extraordinary commitment for exploration and invention of many, and such people would always be remembered with respect and gratitude. In fact such people became examples to demonstrate how intellect must be used to serve the mankind.

The final result however was that a new class came into existence. This new class thrived and is thriving even today, with much greater power and much more wealth. This new class even manipulated the 'democratic rulers' of this world. They have created an intelligence that governs the world. This intelligence exploits and misguides both, the one who puts in honest labour for his survival and also those whose intellectual pursuits are for development of knowledge without any motives of exploiting others. This intelligence is the outcome of human **greed**. It is founded on untruth. It is 'anti-divine'. It is so contagious that it has started seeping into the spiritual and religious thoughts. It was the influence of this intelligence that the moment British decided to leave India, many of the followers of Gandhi wrote him off.

> *Today machinery helps a few to ride on the backs of millions.*

> **(Mahatma;**
> **D.G. Tendulkar)**

> *The saving of the labour of the individual should be the object and honest humanitarian consideration, and not greed, the motive.*

> **(The Collected Works of Mahatma Gandhi)**

There is no point in diluting views of Gandhi on use of machines and automation. By and large he was against automation. He did not oppose that part of industrialization that helped the people. For example, he never suggested any kind of reversal in production of steel. However, he would have definitely opposed any steel industry that mechanized the jobs that gave occupation to blacksmiths.

After his return from South Africa he was primarily concerned about India. Unlike many others, freedom of India was not his only goal as he knew that the real objective was reconstructing India. Further, he was very clear that freedom for India had little meaning if it had to be mere transfer of power from British hands to Indian hands. He never thought of solving India's problems by adopting a route of industrialization; that is sure. He often spoke about India taking a lead in solving its problem of poverty so that it becomes an example for the rest of the world. This confirms that he had in mind to ensure that the approaches he was thinking of were implemented in real earnestness and dedication. He was not averse to making any modifications in his approaches as long as the basic principles of truth and non-violence are not sacrificed. Gandhi was not the man who would have sent all steam engines of railway trains to yards but at the same time he would have definitely asked the railway authorities not to go in for faster trains till other matters that had greater priority were resolved. Those who think that Gandhi wanted to reverse the wheel of progress, in my opinion are, influenced by 'anti-divine' intelligence that I have written about. We need to discuss more on this issue.

> *Where there are millions upon millions of units of idle labour, it is no use thinking of labour saving devices.*

**(Mahatma;
D.G. Tendulkar)**

The farmers in villages and labour forces in towns; the both are only marginally benefitted by innovations. They have to continue to serve the powerful, for their survival. As we know, this power is of two types. First is the physical power that owns or controls the means of production is greedy and violent in nature. Their aim is to satisfy their never ending sensory desires, live in utmost comfort and amass wealth. They are even unmindful of the waste of precious natural resources and the harm they cause to nature and environment. They are generally policymakers. They make such policies that ensure continuation of prevalent condition and even become more favourable to them so that they and their future generations can also live in luxury. Secondly, there are people who use their intellect to serve those in power. They earn their livelihood by 'selling their intellect' without doing any physical labour. Those in power share their income with them (the intelligent ones) in such proportions that they could also afford life of comfort and luxury, if not on par with the powerful ones, but disproportionately very high as compared to farmers and workers that live by sweat of their eyebrows. If we keep aside the question of disproportionate income for the sake of argument and consider only that part of natural wealth that is used by the sections of society which do not earn their livelihood by doing physical labour but which live in great comfort and luxury; then it is easy to find that this economy deprives many others of what is rightfully due to them. The matter does not end here alone. These sections also consume and waste a big chunk of natural wealth causing environmental imbalances and hazardous pollution. They not only have caused much harm to majority of human beings in their life time but also have done, are doing and shall continue to do such deeds that shall endanger all living beings of planet earth in future. About seventy years back when Gandhi was speaking about right livelihood the world had not become that much aware of serious consequences of environmental imbalance and pollution, as it has become now.

> *Farmers must rule our country if we want true democracy in India. There is no need to make them barristers. They should become good farmers, should know how to grow more food, how to keep the land fertile . . . to know all such things is their duty.*

(Harijan Sevak; 12.07.1947)

In the last three chapters we discussed about the necessity of man devoting himself for the welfare of his surrounding; as welfare of all effectively means, man's own good. In remote past wise people insisted that Dharma (duty) must be upheld for the well of mankind. The key thought was, "One who leaves Dharma, falls."

In ancient India and in many of the civilized societies, man presumed that Dharma was the actual ruler; whether the country was ruled by a weak ruler or a strong one, Dharma ultimately found its way. However, the past is gone. The fact is that the vast majority in this world has not been able to get its due share of the progress made possible by human intelligence.

There is every reason to believe that learned people in different societies have always been thinking about the good of mankind. Some tried to find solutions in the history of mankind. They made considerable efforts to analyze and provide some explanations as to why history took a particular route at one place, in particular circumstances at a particular time. They tried to apply themselves after reviewing the history of mankind to find out the right course of action that may be adopted to secure man's future. Others tried to look around and follow others' actions and the outcome of their actions. Then why did it happen that a big majority of people in the world still live under great stress of fulfilling their day to day requirements? Is it because that those who plan for future are seldom free from their **vrittis and prejudices**? Is it because they do not have enough courage to call spades a spade? Or, is it because they feel shy of revealing unorthodox ideas that may not find acceptance by others?

We look at success with awe but discard all failures considering them worthless. We also reveal only that much about us that is considered as success by others and remember only that much about ourselves which we have already revealed. In the affairs concerning mankind we go wrong quite often. It is because of our non-acceptance of failure, as aforesaid, we seldom permit our failures to come on the surface.

In our hearts we know that despite many 'isms' and systems we have tried to use, we have not come any closure to the reality. What have we been doing then? Perhaps, we have been imitating some 'apparent' success and rejoicing.

Societies are also like man. If they have false pride, they will not be able to elevate themselves. They will fall. Like man, societies should also introspect.

I have found that whenever we found some good happening to people it had never been that much because of the system or type of solution that was applied; but because of the strong will to do some good by an individual or more. Humanity will experience a change when more human beings come forward to shoulder their responsibilities. Then, there will be a rule of Dharma.

It needs a detached mind away from success or failure; away from gain or loss; away from fear and greed; with humility tending to zero; to say the following;

> *Labour was a great leveler of all distinctions.*

(Mahatma;D.G. Tendulkar)

With above statement we have come only half way down. In all cultures, those who served by deploying their physical labour, had traditionally been at the bottom of social hierarchy. Slaves, servants, *sevak* . . . all have always been at the bottom. Is it not true that we have been traditionally viewing physical labour as something inferior? It is also true that almost all the societies and cultures have realized the mistake of dividing human beings as superior and inferior and have been trying to instill the values of equality within them. This had been a positive change.

If we look at it impartially we will find that man had not been wrong in considering intellectual ability as something very valuable. After all, man differ from lower species primarily because he is able to think, analyze, plan, decide and act to effect some change that he considers as right. He can distinguish right from wrong. The only problem is that his 'desires' can ride on his intellect and may compel him to move in the wrong direction. Why did Rishis decided to live in hills or jungles away from towns and villages? They did so to distance themselves from the 'objects' of desires. Some may think that Gandhi's intention was to seal man's capacities to 'earn' the objects of desire, at some level, to restrain man's greed. None of Gandhi's speeches or writings suggests that he ever thought of restraining man's intellectual or physical abilities in any way. It must have been evolved from the thought that when God had granted different faculties to man to help him live his life; then why a system of 'balanced use' of the two faculties, mental and physical, should not be there? Historically, man has used his intellectual abilities for spiritual growth as well as his physical progress. In past violent minds made use of their physical strengths to exploit others because then man had not made enough use of his intellectual abilities. Now, when man has made much use of his intellectual abilities, the gains of discoveries and inventions are being used by those violent minds who had acquired disproportionate physical strengths earlier. Physical abilities are limited. They cannot cause that much damage to mankind as unlimited intellectual abilities in the hands of violent exploiters can. This is a phenomenon of modern times. Obviously, humanity is in danger. It has been sufficiently proved that physical and mental wellness is essential for happy living. For mental wellness creative and constructive temperament is a must. There is no rationale behind making use of destructive intellect for some comforts, conveniences and satisfaction of desires by a few, which cause harm to both, the exploited and the exploiters.

We know that those who invented, they did it with good intentions to help the man. But when it came to using the products of man's intelligence, those who had acquired power by violent means manipulated it to their advantage. We have already seen that these violent people have forced a vast majority of human beings to live a life where they have to put in great physical efforts to make even small earning for their survival.

The conditions within these two groups are also not very good. We find that in the section of small population of well to do people, there is much competition with each other to make good money by using their intellect. There are limited opportunities, limited markets, limited jobs or work assignments. Only a few gain and others spend their days in frustration. At the root of coming into existence of the former section had been excessive desires and greed. Although this section is living in luxury having snatched away the legitimate rights of the large population; greed continues to operate within it. Members compete with each other fiercely. There is fear, avarice, hatred, pride arrogance, malice and all such qualities that degrade and devalue life.

Big populations of have-nots are more driven by need than greed. They are generally docile like all those who are accustomed of serving. They compete with each other to satisfy their individual needs, but they are also sympathetic to the needs of others and often co-operate with each other. They can bear a lot and for a long time. However, they can tolerate up to a limit, beyond it they may become violent. Farmers, by habit are more patient, less greedy and less violent. As against this urban industrial workers can be easily aroused. Unemployed from urban regions are more prone to adopt the path of crime.

There had been disparities in past, but the value systems protected the individuals and societies. Industrialization has harmed the value systems; individuals have become lonelier, less tolerant and more aggressive and find the objects of envy existing close by. Possibilities of high rate of crime, large scale violence or circumstances leading to degeneration of society in long run; cannot be ruled out.

The least damage that is being caused by the disparities between those who merely survive by doing physical labour and those who live in comfort by selling their intellect is further degradation of physical labour.

Intellectual activity complements physical labour. That is how the God has made the man.

> *More our life styles differ from that of the farmers more sickly we are likely to be . . . . Man must do physical labour eight hours a day and that too in a manner that our intellectual faculties also get occupied there with.*

> **(Aarogya Sadhan;**
> **M.K.Gandhi, Navjeevan Trust)**

Physical work where intellectual capacities get occupied could only be possible if one does some productive work physically. Gandhi's thoughts were very positive in this respect. It is our experience that when some manual productive work is done by someone with high intellectual ability the output is much better, especially in its quality.

The issue of right livelihood is becoming more and more critical day by day.

25

SPINNING WHEEL—A CONCEPT

My machinery must be the most elementary type which I can put in the home of millions.

(Mahatma; D.G.Tendulkar)

The spinning wheel is itself an exquisite piece of machinery. My head daily bows in reverence to its unknown inventor.

(The Collected Works of Mahatma Gandhi)

While this 'machine age' will go on trying to convert man into machine, I shall go on trying to transform life-less man back into lively human beings.

(Harijan Sevak; 08.29.1926)

The ugly part of man's history is soaked with human blood and stinks of dead human flesh. It is generally a history of wars and destruction. However, there had been occasions when some great ideas were generated that had the potential of adding much value to human life. When

British ruled India, they exported cotton from India at a low price to England to rejuvenate British textile industry that was in trouble. They dumped Indian market with cheap cloth from British Textile (spinning and weaving) mills. The Indian weavers, whose hand weaved cloth was much in demand due to its fine quality, suffered heavily. The British intended to revive their industry by ruining Indian cottage Industry. They were successful.

Gandhi had a unique idea. He thought of crores of Indian farmers who were unemployed or underemployed for the most parts of season. He imagined that if there was small hand operated machine for spinning yarn from cotton which even poor farmers could afford to own and operate; poverty stricken rural India will start vibrating with self confidence. *Charkha* (spinning wheel) was found to exist in some form in some village. After some modification it was introduced. This spinning wheel was an answer to British colonialism. It was a means of production that the operator himself owned. Anyone could spin yarn from cotton during his spare time that added to his income. By practice he could spin fine yarn and earn more.

This could provide occupation to women-folk to make them economically independent. The cloth produced by hand spun and hand woven cotton yarn is called Khadi. The production cost of Khadi was more than mill spun cloth, but the extra cost was to be paid by the people of India to the poor people of India.

I have often said that if we have to give new life to our seven lacs of villages and establish a culture of peace then we have to make Charkha (spinning wheel) the central point of all handicrafts and cottage industries. My trust on Charkha is increasing day by day . . . . I will go a step forward and say that just as we try to discover new stars we must try to keep on searching for new cottage industries.

(Haripura Harijan Sevak; 02.19.1938)

The essence of previous chapter was that man must make balanced use of his intellect and body for earning his livelihood. If we use machines we may go on multiplying our production capacity, thereby reducing employment opportunities for many. Those who own machines will multiply their wealth and may continue submitting themselves more and more to greed and meaningless luxurious life. On the other side a vast majority of people will be left to struggle for survival due to lack of opportunities for gainful employment. Cottage industry is a path of true freedom for the smallest human being. Such industries not only provide opportunities for physical labour for earning one's livelihood but also offer him challenges to use his intellectual capacity for making advancements. Inventions and discoveries must benefit the entire humanity, not merely a class of people.

Food and clothes, these two are essential for life and they shall be so in future also. Life shall become difficult if their availability cannot be relied upon. If a society wants to protect itself non-violently against external invasion or internal fights; it must ensure that its people are self-dependent. Just as we grow and cook our food, we must spin yarn for our clothes.

(Harijan Sevak; 01.13.1940)

Every house should have a Charkha and every village should have at least one Karagha (loom). This is ideal for self-dependence of a village. People in villages must produce their Khadi themselves.

(Harijan Sevak; 09.20.1935)

Crores of people cannot operate mills, they cannot do many jobs, but they can spin. Charkha is like our scriptures, it is economics and also non-violence; all in one.

(Harijan Sevak; 12.21.1947)

The work of Khadi is just like the work of untouchability. It is unimaginable to think how much the people of higher classes have neglected the people of lower classes. The net result of their neglect and insults have been that the poor forgot the art of living . . . . The purpose of Khadi is to rectify the error committed by higher classes by inviting them to do the job of Khadi and asking them to repent by involving themselves in it.

(Harijan Sevak; 07.19.1935)

It is difficult to find instances in human history where the privileged endeavoured to identify the root cause of predicament of the poor masses. The rich did not become rich by chance. They became rich by choice. In most cases they became rich by using violence. Different theories that were evolved suggested that violence of past can be rectified by violent means. Gandhi thought that this solution was defective. Gandhi could see that if mechanization or automation was not made to synchronize with the laws of nature; their use was inherently violent. Just by snatching away the ownership and control of machines from the few who were in power and giving it to masses, the basic defect cannot be removed. Violence, by nature is destructive. It does not construct, it destroys.

Violence is easy. When the objective is to destroy, who is bothered whether left is destroyed first or the right.

Non-violence is constructive. It needs care and attention. To defeat the powerful violent giant who is up to deprive us of our right to use our body to earn our livelihood, the first thing we must do is to make ourselves strong by ensuring that our basic needs like food and cloth are satisfied and then to build our strength by becoming united like a family. All this can be done when we concentrate on our immediate surroundings. Our immediate surroundings start from our villages, nearby villages, our district, and our state and finally, it shall automatically cover our nation. During this journey we do not compete with each other. We support each other and empower each other.

> . . . *Economics of Khadi is different from ordinary economics. Principles of ordinary economics are primarily based on competitive pursuits with marginally small elements of humanity and love for one's own country . . . . whereas economics of Khadi is founded on humanitarian principles and love for one's nation.*

> **(Harijan Sevak; 07.30.1938)**

> *If we have not understood the true meaning of Khadi, many of the efforts we make have little meaning. If thirty crores of Indians have to cover their bodies; then why should they cover it with cloth made in the mills of Paris or Ahmedabad; why*

should they not wear Khadi made with the hands of Daridranarayan?

. . . Whatever you do you should do it for India, not for me . . . . Khadi will stay even after me. This is swarajya; this is swatantrata.

(Harijan Sevak; 02.26.1938)

How far the Indian leaders, the followers of Gandhi, who ruled India, after independence understood the meaning of Charkha and Khadi? I shall give them negative marks.

With the help of Khadi we were trying that instead of the machines driven by steam or electricity, riding over the man; man rode over the machines. With the help of Khadi we were trying that the gap between rich and poor; and big and small is reduced and all men and women live like equals . . . . Whatever we did in last thirty years was not moving backwards.

(Harijan Sevak; 12.21.1947)

Just after four months of India attaining freedom Gandhi had to tell those who decided to rule India that in last thirty years India had not been made to move backwards. I have occasionally tried to highlight such issues that show that many of Gandhi's followers (especially those who ruled India after the British) hardly understood what he had to say. Their only goal was to see that British rule ends. Gandhi, very frequently and repeatedly explained all about, **truth, non-violence, shraddha, swatantrata, swarajya, right livelihood, right conduct, selfless service, khadi** etc. but we hardly find that anybody was trying to carry his work forward. Gandhi spoke about *rajya-dharma (duties to be performed by the one who takes upon himself to serve the people)* but his followers who took the reins in their hands were centered on *rajyadhikar (authority to rule)*. We must listen to Gandhi directly to know what he intended to say.

> *Message of Khadi can penetrate to the remotest of village if we only will that it shall be so.*

> **(Mahatma; D.G. Tendulkar)**

> *If we have Khadi spirit in us, then we should surround ourselves with simplicity in every walk of life.*

> **(Mahatma; D.G. Tendulkar)**

> *Khadi is an activity that absorbs all the time of all the men and women and grown up children if they have faith.*

> **(The Collected Works of Mahatma Gandhi)**

26

RELIGION

Every religion, if it has to be full of life, must have inherent strength to rejuvenate itself.

(Harijan Sevak; 10.05.1935)

Every religion has played its role in the growth of mankind. I consider all great religions as branches of the same tree; each may be different from the rest but they all belong to the same tree.

(Harijan Sevak; 01.28.1939)

Just as my religion is true for me; other religions are also true for their followers.

(Harijan Sevak; 10.05.1935)

If I have the power to make laws, I shall ban all conversions from one religion to another. They become cause of hatred, strife and malice between leaders, representatives and followers of different religions. I will welcome people from

different religions coming from different
nations with pure feelings and mission of
selfless service.

(Harijan Sevak; 05.17.1935)

Gandhi had devotedly surrendered himself to the Supreme
power who was the cause of this infinite universe. His
surrender was complete; it was an emotional compulsion,
intellectual conviction and his rigorous practices of
righteous conduct through his heart, speech and action.
Notwithstanding all this Gandhi has many critics
who consider him a big failure in matters of religion
because India was divided in two parts on communal
(religious) lines at the time of its freedom and in spite of
his best efforts (that includes giving away his own life).
Irrespective of the modern liberal and democratic thoughts
the world is proud of, we still watch with pain, much
violence caused by people having differences in faiths,
thoughts and ritualistic practices. The chapter on religion
has been included in this book because the problem still
persists and the humanity is yet not relieved of its burden.
If I simply highlight the qualities of Gandhi as a religious
human being that would not serve any purpose. I will
attempt to go a little more deep.

We are aware that religious intolerance is still causing
much harm to India and the world. From what we
understand by using the word religion, it is very difficult to
understand as to how followers or leaders of any religion
could be intolerant of any other religion. There could be

only two possibilities. Either those who call them religious are not actually religious or what we understand by the word religion is flawed. I feel that it is best to leave it on leaders and followers of any religion to introspect and decide whether the path they are adopting is a religious path. I am aware that it is not a solution but it definitely is an underlying principle to start with.

In this chapter I shall make an attempt to clarify Gandhi's views on religion. Ancient Indian philosophers accept existence of a supreme power that controls the world. This supreme power is called *Eeshwar* or *Param-atma.* The stay of living beings in this world is for a limited period. This stay is full of suffering and pain. Therefore the objective of their life is to get dissolved in the Supreme existence or become one with the God. This is called *Moksha, Mukti* or *Nirvana.* Whatever good or bad we do, that goes in our account. Bad or sinful deeds are the obstacles in path of *moksha.* Taking birth as human being is a great opportunity, because by using his intellect and body he can do many good deeds to compensate for sins of earlier births. Man is of unstable mind and gets attached to this world despite knowing full well that he has to die sooner or later. His worldly desires know no end. Man's mind and desires lure him to adopt sinful path. He satisfies his sensory desires and derives momentary pleasure. He not only wastes his time but may also cause harm to others in order to seek temporary pleasures for himself. If a lifetime as human being is wasted it amounts to losing an opportunity of salvation and eternal bliss. Indian philosophers have considered God as invisible, indescribable, one who is not born, one who shall not end, unreachable, who has all powers, one who is benevolent for all, one who takes care of all and so on and so forth.

Three paths have been suggested to realize God. First path is of complete devotion and surrender to God. For this one has to detach himself from all worldly pleasures and desires and surrender to the God completely. One who has detached himself from all worldly needs and desires can not cause any harm to any creature in this world. Such person cannot keep himself or for that matter anybody at the centre because he keeps God at the centre of everything. Such people are called *Bhaktiyogi*. *Bhaktiyog* is considered relatively easy because *Bhaktiyogi* does not have to become completely detached from the world; he has to become completely attached to the God and desire Him alone. God becomes the sole object of his love, to which a *Bhaktiyogi* surrenders.

The second path is of knowledge. It is knowledge of truth. Knowledge of the essence of what is real and knowing what is not real. One has to understand the difference between reality and illusion through penance. The knowledge ultimately leads one to the Supreme as He is the only truth and truth is the only reality. This path, called *Jnanayog,* is considered a tough path as it necessitates; able teachers, great amount of discipline, complete detachment, deep contemplation etc.

Ancient Indian scriptures do not leave the mankind alone. They provide enough guidance to him as to how he must conduct himself living his life in different roles and in different capacities. These scriptures can be interpreted by the learned and the wise and leave enough scope for implementing practical modifications according to time, space and circumstances. The duties one must perform according to whatever his position may be in the society, as defined in scriptures, are collectively called *Dharma. The laws of Dharma by* themselves are not *divine laws*; they are laws of worldly conduct framed according to *divine laws*. The laws of Dharma are for the welfare of the universe and strictly avoid any harm even to the smallest particle of the universe. Ancient Indian philosophers have placed highest importance to the *one-ness of the entire existence.* Man who has freedom to act, unlike smaller species that are bound by their instincts; must conduct himself according to Dharma (for the welfare of the universe) because that is considered as the only way to lead a purposeful life. By living life in right manner one is helped in attaining salvation (*moksha*). Geeta suggests the path of selfless action (actions not in one's self interest but in the interest of the *unified whole*) as the third path for *moksha.* This path is of action without any desire for fruits of the action. It is called *Karmayog.*

Ancient Indian philosophy is somewhat different from many other philosophies. It covers science and art of life. There are two parts. The **Darshan** (how to view the truth in things, i.e. philosophy); and the second is **Dharma** (duty). It informs, it presents views of the learned and selfless Rishis and great thinkers, and it presents arguments to help the scholar who studies them to go into the depths of true knowledge. The key thought is that the concepts of *Eeshwar and satya* (the God and the absolute truth) are not easy enough to be understood by human intellect that may be clouded by illusions; and hence each one must be given an opportunity to understand God and truth in his own way. The ancient Indian scriptures do not prescribe or insist on any method of worship or form of God. It opines that one should have faith in God because it helps him, but it does not even insist that one must believe in God's existence.

I have briefly tried to write something about what is popularly known as *Hindu Dharma*. There is nothing like Hindu Religion. In fact, there is no word parallel to 'religion' in Sanskrit or any of the Indian languages. However, there may be many who may be worshipping some Deities, who are believed to have existed in history and by virtue of their exemplary conducts (according to popular belief) command revered positions. Many faiths exist under the large umbrella of ancient Indian thought. The ancient Indian thought always supersedes and controls the smaller faiths. While describing the above I had not been under any pressure that I might go wrong. I wrote it in good faith, and that was enough. Ancient Indian philosophy gives enough freedom of thought.

I find that throughout his life Gandhi relied upon his own conscience and took advantage of ancient Indian thoughts for finding answers to his questions about right and wrong.

I have no hesitation in saying that in his efforts to purify and enrich his thoughts with the help of ancient Indian philosophy Gandhi, unknowingly, made valuable contribution in some principles of *Hindu Dharma.*

Gandhi strongly believed that Dharma and similarly, practical truth has to be modified according to the needs of the universe from time to time, at different locations and at different circumstances.

> *The religion that has narrow outlook and that does not appear to human intellect as conforming to the truth; shall not be found useful in building a new society based on perfect human values. Everything shall be valued differently in the new society we are thinking of. Man shall be valued according to his character and not according to his wealth, status in the society or the lineage.*

(Harijan Sevak; 03.08.1942)

> *These temples are bridges between the invisible, incomprehensible, indescribable and eternal God and the man with infinite limitations. All of us cannot become great thinkers of truth. We are made of earth. We are born on this earth hence our minds are attached to the earth. How can we derive satisfaction by thinking of someone whom*

we have never seen and who is without any form? We desire something that we can see, touch or with which we can feel some closeness. That may be a book, or an idol carved out of stone or may be some clean, peaceful open space. People of different religions have different symbols that they can concentrate on for remembering God.

We should not go to temples with a doubt in mind as to how can God exist in a stone. We should have shraddha, complete faith that the God who exist everywhere is also there in the temple. If we have that faith, we shall find that our shraddha for the God, the source of all energy, shall go on increasing day by day.

(Harijan Sevak; 01.30.1937)

In my opinion the temples of Hindus are not sacred abode of the God till all Hindus without any discrimination are not entitled to worship God. In Hindu Dharma there is no distinction between small and big. Everybody is equal in the eyes of God. All religions are under scrutiny to confirm if they uphold the principles of equality. I want that Hindu religion must pass with full marks.

(Harijan Sevak; 07.27.1947)

To develop a clearer understanding, let us view the matter of religion in two parts. Let us begin with a belief that our life has a meaning and a specific purpose. Let us have a faith that we are not without a cause and our life on this earth is only a short life form out of our eternal existence. The faith that we do not actually die, makes many things simple for us. The knowledge that the life form we adopt when we are born on this earth is very important; gives meaning to our life. When we realize that it shall depends on our efforts in this life span as to how soon we will be able to attain a state of eternal happiness, we are able to attach necessary urgency for generating appropriate thoughts and taking right actions. We are not aware of our life before or beyond the present life span; we do not know if our present life is connected with some reality; but having faith in the phenomena as referred earlier, on the basis of the words spoken by our forefathers, do not restrict or restrain us, instead it greatly empower us. There are many thoughts regarding reality of our existence and our true nature that we may classify under the branch of spirituality. It is almost certain that Gandhi was convinced with the thoughts contained in ancient Indian philosophy. His extraordinary bent towards non-violence, kindness and forgiveness came from Christianity and Jain Dharma. Gandhi stuck to selfless service for the benefit of others; a highly valuable thought of *Nishkam Karma* or *Akarma* of Geeta. He chanted *Ramanama to* seek support of God in his ventures and for helping him to arrive at correct decisions. In the language of modern world that breaths not on air but information; Gandhi was a thoroughly connected person. He was simultaneously connected to the God, the World and himself. That was his religion.

I often come across people who almost ridicule Gandhi for his insistence on non-violence. Some quote from scriptures to suggest that violence has a proper place in ancient Indian scriptures. The scriptures have allowed destruction by the will of God or Godlike beings. They have not justified violence by human beings. In fact the ancient Indian thought related ultimate truth to non-violence. However, the place of Dharma (sacred duty) in human life was considered supreme and the Indian philosophy was very clear that if Dharma itself became weak, the violence of all kinds would prevail in this world. It was therefore believed that Dharma must be protected at any cost so that non-violence rules the world. I am also not saying that Gandhi differed from ancient Indian philosophy in the sense that he gave any less importance to Dharma. Principle of *Satyagraha,* that is insistence for truth, was insistence for Dharma. The difference lies in the fact that Gandhi did not accept the cost of violence for protecting or installing Dharma. Even in extreme situations he preferred to err on the safer side. He often spoke of making ultimate sacrifice, which is, giving away one's own life for the cause of truth. "Don't kill. If killing is inevitable, kill yourself."Gandhi often intended to say. That was Gandhi's religion.

There is no doubt that whenever we begin to think about the ultimate meaning and purpose of our lives and about our connection with some unknown reality, we cannot avoid placing our existing physical life at the centre of our thought process. This exactly is the source of all religions that exist in this world. Religions are not merely a few codes of conduct, cultures that have been formed with passage of time, some practices people of different races follow or some rituals that bind a few people together. If and when, all the above along with many more of such things taken together get connected with the thought of ultimate reality of life; different religious systems are evolved. Religion is some kind of rope we voluntarily like to bind ourselves with to avoid being thrown away from us and away from the God, into a void; we do not know anything about. The great souls who had gained some knowledge about human life had woven the ropes of religion so that people spend their life together sharing with each other what they had, without causing harm to fellow beings and doing all such acts that preserve life and not doing things that endangered it.

> *In fact all our deeds must be completely guided by religion. Religions cannot be sects confined to narrow paths. Religions imply shraddha in refined systems of morality for the entire world. If the Unknown we are seeking is not visible to us and we cannot properly understand Him; it does not mean that He becomes less real in any way. The religion I am speaking about may be beyond Hindu religion, Islam, Christianity or all other religions, but it also does not negate them.*

The truth is that it takes all religions in its fold and evolves a real religion.

(Harijan Sevak; 02.10.1940)

As such religion is an individual affair. True religion should help us in making our lives virtuous using whatever light we have been able to receive; giving away to others the most precious of possessions we have; thereby joining with the human race in its efforts to realize the ultimate reality, the God.

. . . All great religions are basically same. We must have a natural respect for other religions just as we respect our own religion.

(Harijan Sevak; 11.28.1936)

Gandhi was completely against all such things in any religion that did not conform to his concept of truth and non-violence. Apart from his philosophical orientation towards ancient Indian philosophy he called himself a traditional Hindu, *Sanatani Hindu.* He prayed to God everyday and even repeated the name of God with the help of prayer beads, but he had no temple in his *Ashram,* not even a separate room for offering prayers what to speak of having any idols for worshipping. The collective prayers in Gandhi's *Ashram* included prayers of different religions because he desired that all must also respect others' religions apart from their own religions.

> *"Satyannasti paro dharmah" and "Ahimsa paramo dharmah", the meaning of the word 'dharma' is different in these two sayings. The first says, 'There is no goal other than truth' and the second means, 'There is no dharma greater than non-violence'. One can worship truth while being completely engrossed in his duties. . . . If one has to witness ruin of his country for holding on to the truth, he must opt for the truth. If one has to leave his country for sticking to the truth, he must go for the truth.*

> **(Gandhi Seva Sangh; Savali, 03.03.1936)**

> *There are several castes and tribes. They all are manmade. They also keep on changing. Old ones vanish and new ones come up. There are several castes based on professions of people or the way they earn their livelihood. It is only in India that I have found very peculiar ways of discrimination. Those belonging to higher caste do not marry in lower castes or not eat with them. There are practices that intellect fails to understand. These*

practices are damaging to growth of people. These practices have no relation with religion. . . . There is a great need to do away with illogical and inhuman restrictions. If this is done then such type of distinction will vanish and Hindu religion will return to its glory. That will also be good for the world.

(Harijan Sevak; 01.25.1936)

I feel Gandhi was very fair and impartial about the apparent differences between different religions. There is no doubt that he wanted to see his own religion without any blemishes. To get rid of defects in Hindu religion he launched extra-ordinary constructive programs and reformist movements. This is not difficult to understand. In fact Hindu population in India had always been in majority. If its defects were taken care of that could have benefited the nation. Further, Gandhi knew that the Hindu religion had some very special qualities that did not permit easy proliferation of violence; hence strength of Hindu religion could have benefitted the humanity itself.

Gandhi was completely against people relinquishing their own religions and joining other religious sects. He strongly loved his religion. He did not accept those parts of Hindu religion that, according to him, did not conform to truth and non-violence. He worked against them in an organized manner throughout his life. Through his actions he gave a message to all that one must endeavour to remove shortcoming of his own religion instead of highlighting virtues of one's own religion and defects of others' religions.

> *If one claims that one part of God is superior to another, it would amount to revolting against the God. Irrespective of differences in height, colour of skin, shape, virtues or shortcomings, human beings cannot be discriminated as superior or inferior. No doubt there are apparent differences between teacher-pupil, servant-master, and criminal-judge but . . . if one considers himself superior to the other, it cannot be viewed as the right conduct. Most of the pain existing in the world is caused by the thought of inequality. When high caste Hindus consider themselves superior to lower caste ones, they carry the thought of distinction very far. If serving others is our goal, we must introspect deeply and should wash away our old sins of untouchability.*

> **(Harijan Sevak; 02.22.1935)**

> *Ancient Indian scriptures and to the best of my knowledge, the Christian scriptures say that the God loves those who are discarded and neglected by the world. In*

this respect only the low caste people, who have been neglected by the society due to its false pride and worthless arrogance, deserve to be called 'Harijan' (men of God).

(Harijan Sevak; 08.22.1936)

Gandhi had been very precise and specific about the qualities of Dharma installed by ancient Indian scriptures.

Elevated status of Hindu Dharma depends on truth and non-violence; that exactly is the reason why Hindu Dharma cannot have any enmity with anyone. Hindu Dharma must cherish the idea that all the glorified religions of the world must progress further to ensure peaceful growth and development of the world.

(Harijan Sevak; 03.25.1939)

Basic qualities of Hindu Dharma had been its exceptional tolerance and its ability of assimilating the good qualities of all who came in its contact.

(Harijan Sevak; 09.28.1947)

Following three quotations of Gandhi almost summarize views of Gandhi on religion.

Whatever one is able to internalize through his heart becomes his religion.

(The Diary of Mahadev Desai; Editor, N.D. Parikh)

Worship of whatever kind if truthfully done putting the heart into it, is equally fruitful for all . . . . God does not pay attention to the words or methods of worship, He only sees through our deeds and intent of spoken words.

(The Diary of Mahadev Desai; Editor, N.D. Parikh)

The practice of truth and non-violence melts religious differences, and we learn to see beauty in each religion.

(Mahatma; D.G. Tendulkar)

This chapter on religion shall remain incomplete if I do not present views of Gandhi on scriptures. Sanskrit word for scriptures is **shastra**. There are numerous references that advice mankind to conduct according to **shastra.** Gandhi said;

Shastras are not merely something written, as books are. They must have life. Shastras must be statements or sayings of some highly learned wise person with impeachable character having no difference in his actions and words. If we are not able to catch hold of something of this kind then whatever appears to be true to us can become a Shastra for us provided we have proper sanskaras.

**(The Diary of Mahadev Desai;
Editor, N.D. Parikh)**

The word *sanskara* needs some explanation. As such *sanskara* means upbringing. However, ancient Indian thoughts give substantial importance to the man's characters of earlier births. Practically it can be said that one who has lived with good people in childhood, is good by nature and has been taught and trained to be good ; has good *sanskara*. This statement of Gandhi must be connected to Gandhi's insistence on 'sticking to truth'. We need to make many sacrifices to internalize truth. Similarly, we have to overcome many temptations, win over many hurdles and may have to pay heavy prices before we can conclusively say that, in general, we are likely to behave in a right manner, irrespective of the circumstances.

Revelation of spiritual subjects cannot be done with ordinary methods. They can be revealed through actions that exactly matched with the related spiritual thought. In my opinion spiritual scriptures influence a seeker (impart knowledge to a willing student of spirituality) in two ways. Firstly, the scriptures must reveal true history of the writer's (creator or revealer) experiences; and secondly, the conduct of the disciples or devotees of the writer must have been according to the preaching and teachings of the writer. The writers of scriptures give life to the scriptures and the disciples of those writers nurture the scriptures with their conduct.

(Harijan Sevak; 12.16.1939)

I find this quotation very meaningful. It is often said that scriptures were revealed by the God himself or some Deities. I have noticed that Gandhi always had a great respect for all kinds of faiths that mankind had, provided they did not cause any harm to anybody, that is, they were non-violent. Here the meaning of the word faith must be taken as **shraddha.** In the above quotation Gandhi considers the scriptures as product of pure and meaningful expressions of spiritual experiences that were radiated by the writers; and were received and internalized by their followers; and the outcome was in form of conduct of the followers, which were also spiritual experiences. If any creation satisfies the above condition, it could be considered as *shastra.* Needless to say, that content of any scripture has to be true, beneficial for all and hence divine. I give below one more quotation from Gandhi which I consider important.

Shastras that have scope for revisions and changes according to the needs of time are shastras in true sense. If shastras have to remain as guiding forces for human lives, they will have to change with time and grow. There are very few principles that never change and continue to guide us at all times. Scriptures are not needed to explain them. In fact scriptures are written on the basis of principles that do not change.

(Harijan Sevak; 08.03.1947)

In the above quote Gandhi is referring to necessity of openness in religions. This kind of openness is clearly visible in contributions made by learned Rishis of ancient India. One finds various streams of thoughts flowing from learned Rishis on the basis of their deep contemplation and experiences. Hindu thought accepts necessity of changes according to time, place and circumstances. In ancient India a system of *shastrarth* was popular; whereby open arguments on the intent and contents of *shastras* were held between the learned Rishis. Such *shastrarthas* were highly welcome. This is a scientific way of dealing with any knowledge; whether physical or spiritual.

27

OUR SOCIETY AND SOCIAL REFORMS

❧❦❧

Willing submission to social restraint for the sake of the well-being of the whole society enriches both the individual and the society of which he is a member.

(Mahatma; D.G. Tendulkar)

How will a social reformer decide what is the right time to act? He has to rely on his faith otherwise he may be called 'a person in great hurry' or fearful or lazy. One should listen to his disciplined inner-voice and act making truth and non-violence as his shield. A reformer cannot act otherwise.

(Mahatma Gandhi in England; Mahadev Desai)

The first quotation needs to be well understood. Gandhi has qualified the expression *'willing submission to social restraint'*; by making it necessary *'for the sake of the well-being of whole society'*. The question arises whether the society has some kind of mechanism which ensures that the restraints imposed by it are for the well-being of the whole society? That is not an absolute impossibility; but for that any society shall have to undergo several reforms to develop sufficient number of individuals who are vigilant to notice when any custom starts causing harm and act to remedy the situation. Such individuals will not only be aware and concerned about the well being of members of the society, but they will also possess temperament for selfless service. For all practical purposes we can say that role of social reformers will remain very important for a sufficiently long time. The way the world has changed over the years man has also been affected on many counts by sticking to undesired social norms and evading desired social practices.

> *Goodness lives on its own strength, not the evil. Evil grows in the neighbourhood of good, survives on it and even thrives on it. When the support of the good is pulled away from the evil, evil dies its own death. Even if we are not able to change the hearts of the evil people who cause harm to the society, we must make them realize that they are not acceptable to the good people who are making their place in the society.*

(Harijan Sevak; 09.14.1947)

The rowdy, indecent, uncultured, evil minded and violent elements of the society do not descend from the sky or suddenly appear from within the earth; they are the products of the ills that exist in our society. Our society is responsible for their existence. They are like some disease whose cause must be identified with a view to curing it.

(Harijan Sevak; 06.14.1940)

If we refuse to listen to what our opponent has to say or make fun of him after listening to him then it means that we are no longer ready to act reasonably. Intolerance hampers our ability to recognize truth. If God has granted us limited ability to understand and reason out, it becomes our duty to move ahead courageously with our inner strength. However, we must always keep our mind open and be ready to face consequences if we misjudge the truth. By keeping our mind open we may be able to keep on continuously verifying if our understanding of truth is not very much off the mark and also making efforts to gradually get rid of the blemishes if and when they are identified. It is impossible to uphold the principle of democracy with close minds and intolerant attitude.

(Harijan Sevak; 05.31.1942)

Gandhi could not turn his face the other way whenever and wherever he noticed any injustice. He did something about it or at least raised his voice against it. It will be more appropriate to say that something from deep within him compelled him, to view the injustice or the harm that was being caused to any component of humanity, in relation to his concepts of truth and non-violence; and thereafter express himself in some form. He experimented and expressed about his findings in matters of desirable human behavior, physical and mental health, individual and collective wisdom, individual and collective prayers, organizations and organizational behaviour and all that influenced human life whether considered as significant or insignificant by others.

This is a fact that the things that appear to be big to others do not appear to me as big as they are thought to be; and many things normally considered as insignificant become very important for me.

(The Diary of Mahadev Desai; Editor, N.D. Parikh)

I belong to the God. He makes me dance. I dance to his tune. I am not worried about my life . . . . I am playing with my life.

(The Diary of Mahadev Desai; Editor, N.D. Parikh)

I also give below a few more quotations from Gandhi that surprise me with his infinite receptivity for the pains a living being in this world has to bear and his internal urge to respond to it.

For me life of a goat is not of lesser value than that of a human being. I will not kill a goat for saving my own life. I believe that weaker a living being is, more it becomes entitled for protection and shelter from us, against human violence.

(My Experiments with Truth; M.K. Gandhi)

It is the right of any organization to develop itself into an efficient and strong organization. For this purpose it must frame and impose upon itself rules regulations and terms conditions.

(Harijan Sevak; 01.18.1942)

Maintaining accounts of an organization has no relation with trust or mistrust. To maintain accounts is an independent Dharma by itself.

(Satyagraha in South Africa; M.K. Gandhi)

We can also find Gandhi speaking about very small issues that matter for an ordinary man.

We also call shoes Padtran or Kantkari (that save feet from unfavourable natural conditions like excessive heat, cold or thorns). We should wear shoes only in such unfavourable conditions otherwise it is better to remain barefooted. There also it is better to protect only soles not the entire feet.

(Aarogya Sadhan; M.K. Gandhi)

Just as some sad condition gives pain, some physical disorder (disease) is also expressed through some pain. A disease must be cured. Habit of medication for relief from pain is not only useless but it also causes considerable harm in most cases. Taking medicines for obtaining relief from pain is just like keeping waste and dirt inside our houses covered with the purpose of hiding it . . . . Disease shows that some harmful things have accumulated inside our bodies. Nature has its own ways to clean our bodies . . . we must identify the process through which nature cleans our bodies and must find ways and means to support such process.

(Aarogya Sadhan; M.K. Gandhi)

Methods suggested by shastras (shastra-vidhi) do not mean some rituals to be performed in the name of religion. They are the ways and methods of self discipline and self-control suggested by the learned people of exemplary characters after deep studies, extensive experimentation and experiencing.

(Anaskati Yog; M.K. Gandhi)

Gandhi's views on two particular issues are of immense importance; the caste system in India and the place of women in the society.

We had some discussions on how the high caste people treated the low caste people in India in the chapter *Religion*. Here we will discuss briefly about the caste system. Unlike the intolerance of Hindus and Muslims toward each other's religious practices that had its lows and highs from time to time, discrimination of low caste

Hindus by the high caste ones had been rather consistent for a long period.

The case of religious conflicts is different. Muslims invaded India and ruled over it using brutal force. They even tried to completely tear into pieces the religious fabric of India. In spite of this India took them largely only as invaders to whom they were defeated. Later the two communities coexisted more or less peacefully and accepted each other. It was only under the British rule and that too almost at the end of it that some sections of Muslim population wanted a separate state. Many feel that British caused and designed this division with malicious intent to weaken India to continue their rule in some form, if that was possible. There is no strong logic to suggest that tension between the two communities flared up without reason or without the addition of fuel by some British policy makers, to some feeble spark that might have appeared accidently somewhere. No sane Indian, Hindu or Muslim, including Gandhi could understand as to how and why the peaceful coexistence between the two communities was thwarted. Many tried to diffuse the ugly situation but all failed including Gandhi. Gandhi with his invincible artillery of non-violence fought fiercely and did not permit violence to have the last word. Gandhi did not give away his non-violence; he gave away his life. Today, the ancient Indian thought of Ahimsa (non-violence) survives in India. The after effects of division are still there. But today when a Hindu and a Muslim in India fight with each other there are two Hindus and two Muslims who stop them.

I had started discussing about the caste system but briefly switched over to religious conflict. My purpose was to indicate that the problems associated with caste systems were very different from religious conflict that arose due to demand of separate state. The latter shows that intolerant minds can hardly hold any religious thought. Ancient Indian thinkers prepared Indian soil for years and years by sowing the seeds of tolerance. Several invasions in past robbed India of its wealth but none of them could convert it into a violent nation. This is rather strange that caste system in India existed in a form that looks to be quite inconsistent with spiritual psyche that people of India possess. It will be worthwhile to revisit the historical root of this system.

Ancient Indian civilization categorized people in four castes according to the duties they were expected to perform. First category was that of *Brahmins*, whose profession was to study the scriptures, gain knowledge and impart that knowledge only to those who were entitled to gain that knowledge. The expression, 'those who were entitled to gain that knowledge' is important. It generally meant, for example, that the people who were supposed to earn their livelihood by cleaning of clothes or making earthen pots were not entitled to gain knowledge of *shastras* or strategic warfare. *Brahmins*, by birth, were entitled to adopt the profession of learning highest knowledge and teaching. They commanded maximum respect in the society. Of course, they had to conduct themselves in a manner that made them capable of delivering to the society what was expected from them.

They could impart knowledge of scriptures to others who were *Brahmins* by birth. They could also teach the people of second category, the *Kshatriyas,* (the fighter race) but to gain the highest knowledge the student had to prove that he had become entitled to receive it.

Kings, princes or responsible officers of the kingdom belonged to *Kshatriya* caste. Learned *Brahmins* could become advisers of the kings or the kingdom. *Kshatriyas* were duty bound to protect the people of the kingdom they belonged to and look after their welfare. *The Brahmins* were advisers to the kings or his court. They were duty bound to ensure that people who ruled acted only according to the provisions of Dharma (duty). There are instances when some *Kshatriyas*, having gained highest knowledge or because of their exemplary conduct as kings, commanded equal or even more respect than *Brahmins* of their times. There are also instances when some *Brahmins* became brilliant fighters and became threats to the bravest among *Kashtriyas.*

The third in the hierarchy were *Vaishyas*. Their profession was to do business of all kinds. They had to invest their wealth productively so that necessities of life are available to the people of the kingdom. They were also expected to finance the rulers when the kingdom was in difficulty due to wars or natural calamities. For these services they were entitled to earn reasonable profit for their survival and growth of their wealth.

At the bottom were the people who served the higher castes and earned their livelihood by serving others. They were called *Shudras*. They were not at all entitled to gain knowledge contained in scriptures. They were also not entitled to gain advanced knowledge of using arms or the combat tactics or war strategies, as that remained with *Brahmins* and *Kshatriyas*. In absence of any gadgets or equipments for reduction in labour, methods of personal hygiene and safety of the worker, *Shudras* worked in conditions that could be called sub-human. However, *shudras* remained a part of social system and the society did not neglect them in times of crisis. In olden times all the societies had servants and slaves. Slavery did not exist in Indian system. The kings who defeated other kings ruled over the kingdom of the defeated kings; but the *Kshatriyas* never harmed any unarmed man, women or child, as that was against Dharma. While *Shudras* remained integral part of the society they undoubtedly remained the most discriminated lot with no opportunities to improve their status and lifestyles.

We find that the caste system had several advantages if we view the systems of olden times meant to ensure overall growth of the society. Growth and circulation of knowledge, its proper use and material growth of people along with their physical protection were given the highest priority by ancient Indian thinkers. The two castes *Brahmins* and *Kshatriyas* were duty bound to ensure this for the society and the entire society was duty bound to provide them full support in performance of their duties. These two castes became most important for the society.

It seems that the concept of rebirth and hence the importance of contributions of life experiences from earlier births in formation of human personality and psyche, greatly influenced the ancient Indian thinker in defining social norms in a manner that the two castes, *Brahmin* and *Kshatriya* remain totally committed to their Dharma (duty). They needed to have appropriate *sanskaras* to be firmly bound by their Dharma. It was essential that they came from families who were committed to their Dharma (The protectors needed to come only from *Kshatrya* family, the teachers needed to come from *Brahmin* family); they received appropriate education and training from some able *Gurus* studying with other students who came from similar families; they moved, made friends with and married in families of same caste. In short, for a *Brahmin* or *Kshatriya* blood and upbringing mattered so that they remained uninfluenced by any thought or conduct that distracted them from their duties. For example, death in a battle was a great honour for a *Kshatriya* and hence his wife gave him the sword when he proceeded for battle. There is a proverb in Sanskrit, *Yatha Raja Tatha Praja*. The proverb means the conduct of people depends on the conduct of their king. *Brahmins* were responsible for ensuring that the kings conducted themselves appropriately. The intent of ancient thinkers was that the upper castes remained committed to sacrifices they were expected to make for the society and with pleasure embraced a life of penance for performance of their duties.

Defining one's means of livelihood by birth helped the *vaishyas* and *shudras* also. The training process was automatic in olden times. A carpenter's son learned the nuances of trade from his elders in his family. Generation after generation, the skills improved. Perhaps, the society was a very well knit society. Higher castes were respected but they were also aware of the responsibility they had for the castes that served. Generally there was no hatred for lower castes. They were bound socially and many rituals could not be completed without the involvement of people who served. There are findings that wars caused some important changes in complexion of the caste system. Violence is normally associated with devilish qualities. Weakening of influence of Dharma enhances selfishness, greed, hatred, cruelty, false pride etc. When there were more battles to fight, larger numbers of fighters were needed. Many from the service castes took part in wars and many of them fought brilliantly and were given higher positions in army. These people from castes that served made all attempts to detach themselves from their actual castes and used their power and wealth to make the people of lower castes treat them with respect. The history did a lot to damage the system as it did to religion, culture and way of life. The caste system (*varna-vyavastha*) cannot be assumed to be the same as proposed by the ancient thinkers. One should not forget the fact that Indian history of past one thousand years had been of invasions by so called civilized people and uncivilized people with intention of looting or forcefully making use of resources and wealth of India. They have played havoc with Indian culture, spiritual thoughts, social systems and economic structure. Some destroyed its temples and dumped the books of knowledge into deep seas and others took away its wealth including the wealth of its knowledge and the both forced into India their languages, religions and cultures to ruin India's value systems. They also did the job of distorting its history, intentionally or unintentionally.

Gandhi understood it and responded to it constructively and without any prejudices or malice. He knew that a system which has been completely wrecked needed to be restructured according to democratic norms only. *Ram-rajya* cannot be reinstalled because today's modern society cannot have one Ram with perfect conduct; it can only have many Rams with humanly possible superior conduct.

We often hear phrases like 'social reforms' and 'social engineering', but these phrases are egoistic expressions of very narrow intellectual process. Gandhi wanted that people with non-violent psyche; the psyche that India possessed traditionally thanks to ancient Indian thinkers; should endeavour to restructure Indian society with their own efforts.

> *Varna and Ashram have no relation with caste system. Through Varna-vyavastha we are advised that we must earn our living by working according to our family traditions or what has been allotted to us as our responsibility. This system does not reveal the rights we have. It talks*

about our duties (Dharma) only. And all the duties that have been specified keep the benefit of mankind at the centre. This system also suggested that no work is superior or inferior. All the specified works are equally important.

There is nothing in Varna-vyavastha that provides any basis for treating even some varnas as inferior or superior, what to say of giving inhuman treatment to a few. Hindu Dharma considers truth as God and it has courageously accepted non-violence as a law for human race, that cannot be compromised, come what may.

(Harijan Sevak; 07.18.1036)

We cannot say that any Varna out of the four (Brahmin, Kshatriya, Vaishya or Shoodra) is alive in its true sense. The only option we have is to accept the Dharma of service, the Shoodra Dharma. It does not mean that we should abandon the Dharma of gaining knowledge. We must make all out efforts to gain knowledge; we must become as courageous and as sacrificing as possible; we must work hard to produce more and improve trade. All this must be done with religious outlook and selflessly.

Then, it may become possible that true Brahmins, Kshatriyas or Vaishyas are evolved from amongst us; and all these varnas are reborn without any distinction and malice. When this Varna-Dharma is established all disputes of Communism, Socialism, Congressism, Gandhism and Castism will be vanished.

**(Gandhi Seva Sangh;
Vrindavan, 05.06.1939)**

I believe in earlier births and rebirths. All relations are the outcomes of Sanskaras. The law of God is difficult to understand. It is matter of great research.

(Harijan Sevak; 08.10.1940)

Some explanations are needed in connection with the above quotations. Ancient Indian scriptures described four *Varnas* and four Aashrams. The four *Varnas* (*Brahmins, Kshatriyas, Vaishyas* and *Shoodras*) have already been explained. Four *Ashramas* have been described as *Brahmcharya* (studentship, initial 25 years period, a period of learning); *Grihasth* (25 years period of career and family life from 26th year to 50th year of age); *Vanprstha* (from 51st year to 75th year, when husband and wife leave home and go to forests away from worldly life) and finally, *Sanyas*, when wife returns to home with sons but husband leaves all worldly attachments and strives for attaining *Moksha.*

We find that scriptures defined the occupations and right livelihood which ensured appropriate survival of human beings and maintaining of a society that looked after the collective needs of its members with minimum individual stresses. In this system not only basic human needs and desires were taken care of but there had been a provision for spiritual growth of man. System of *Ashramas* took care of man's need of gaining knowledge of truth and also helped him to lead his worldly life. In this system the human society received youthful contribution from people of the age group of 25 to 50. Society also gained by making use of wisdom of those who had conducted themselves appropriately in their respective lives.

Gandhi clarified in the quotations given above that scriptures advised about the duties and not the rights. If lower castes were looked down upon fault lies elsewhere and to rectify the situation, Gandhi suggested that all types of work; whether intellectual or of taking care of people, of maintaining order in the society, of trade and commerce, or of producing and serving by using physical labour; must be treated equally important for the society, which they actually are. He recommended cleaning the slate and starting afresh according to needs of the modern society. Gandhi never trusted in dealing with falsehood by doing any patch work. He knew that it was counterproductive. Indian constitution provided for ten years period for giving special treatment to lower castes. Sixty-five years have gone since India's constitution became effective; today special treatment and reservations for lower castes is a thriving business for politicians and administrators of India.

Human society has developed the system of democracy. This is a historical reality and is virtually irreversible in modern times. If any human conduct is considered necessary one has no option but to go through the process of democracy to inculcate it.

> *Wherever there is rule of the people, everything must rise upwards from the bottom. Only such rule can last and become glorified by becoming strength of the people.*

(Harijan Sevak; 11.02.1947)

WOMAN

The status of women in *Vaidic* period was high. There is no doubt that the highest honour in Indian society was given to the most learned and wise, who devoted their lives to deep contemplation in solitude to explore the meaning and purpose of life. After gaining true knowledge they established their *Ashrams* away from towns and villages, generally in forests and taught. They were called *Rishis* (male) or *Rishikas* (female). It must have been a tough task as human life was endangered not only by ferocious animals but also by violent and barbaric human races. References are available about approximately 330 *Rishis* and 26 Rishikas. There are a very big number of female deities, some of whom are considered very powerful and fierce fighters. This could not have happened unless women had their independent status and were not considered as commodities in the hand of males. There is no doubt that women have lesser physical strength than men and are vulnerable to be used by men to fulfill their sensual desires. If status of women was high in ancient India it must have been due to well thought and practiced social systems that were in existence in that period. The conditions might have been deteriorated because man is not free from his desires that can make him violent, unconcerned about others and cruel. However, invasion by other races that had no respect for women caused maximum damage to the status of Indian women. It was the lust of these invaders that gave rise to '*Jouhar system*' (when wives burned themselves to death after the death of their husbands), '*Purdah system*' (covering the entire body and face so that males cannot see women), *Dowry-system, Child marriages* and over all lowering of status of woman. At the time of Gandhi the west was supporting the thought that women must have equal opportunities that men had and must be free to compete with men in all endeavours of life.

Gandhi was not a mere 'sympathizer' of women. He told women to empower themselves and become a participant in national building.

There had been mad wars between nations and there had also been wars against insane policies of our societies. Some women think that they must become equal participants with man in handling these wars. I do not agree with this. In my opinion women must have their independent opinion and action plan to deal with or participate in these wars. The women must think like women and not man.

Men have messed up with many situations by applying their violent thoughts in most matters. The world is moving towards a disaster due to men's folly and the men will make the women commit suicide along with them. It is the duty of women to prevent men from committing more mistakes.

(Harijan Sevak; 11.21.1936)

Woman is a symbol of sacrifice and hence that of non-violence. That is why her work must be supportive to peace, not wars. . . . There may not be a legal restriction for women participating in hunting or use of spears for it; but women by nature are not inclined to do such tasks. Woman has been created to complement man.

(Harijan Sevak; 12.02.1931)

Basically man and woman are same. Their souls are same. They lead similar lives. They have similar feelings. One cannot live without the support of another.

(Harijan Sevak; 02.24.1940)

While this is true that man and woman are basically similar, it is equally true that they are structurally different. They have different duties to perform. The majority of women bear children and this will continue forever. The quality needed to perform this duty is to endure, to tolerate. This is mother's Dharma. By nature she rules the house. Man earns for the house. She protects the earnings and distributes it. She takes care in every sense. If she does not take care of human race it will be destroyed.

Except for distribution of work between men and women, other qualities and cultural necessities for both men and women are the same.

(Harijan Sevak; 02.24.1940)

Marriages should never be viewed as commercial transactions. There is a strong relation between system of dowry and caste system. When the numbers of brides or grooms are restricted by availability of a match from same caste the system of dowry shall continue. To get rid of both the evil systems, the young men and women along with their parents must welcome marriages outside their castes. Further, if girls are able to summon enough courage to remain unmarried if suitable matches cannot be found, that will bring revolutionary change in the status of women. Apart from all the above the age of marriages must be revised upwards.

Youth of the country must be given such education that brings about revolutionary changes in their way of thinking and temperament on the above lines.

(Harijan Sevak; 05.23.1936)

The most important thing in Gandhi's opinion about women was their contribution in all aspects of humanity. When women compete with men in the world (which is the outcome of male's perception of human life) their contribution in the affairs of the world would be totally absent. If a woman rules a group of men she does it by overpowering them according to the rules of men. To give an example, if a woman tries to dictate her terms to a group of cruel men, she often does it by becoming crueler than men. That is very undesirable for humanity. Women's job is to make this world less violent and more tolerant. She is tolerant by nature. If she conducts herself according to her nature, the world shall be benefitted. Those men who talk about uplifting women according to their understanding; or those women, who talk of defeating men in their game; are inviting more trouble for the human race. Gandhi wanted that women must honourably conduct themselves in accordance with their true Dharma and in totality.

Gandhi was in favour of celibacy, something that may appear to the world as impractical. However, this message is of great importance from the point of understanding the enormous value of a self-disciplined life with least possible desires. There is no doubt that a world with lesser desires will be a more congenial world for women.

> *A pure and disciplined life had never been a cause of sorrow. Whichever way one may try to deceive him, love and sensual desires are two different things. Love without desires, elevates a man and relationships founded on sensual desires lead to downfall.*

> **(Harijan Sevak; 02.01.1936)**

> *Human life is different from animal life. The rule that must be followed in married life is; do not give birth to a child unless it*

is necessary and do not have an intercourse unless the couple desires to have a child.

(Gandhi Seva Sangh; Savali, 03.06.1936)

Brahmacharya (celibacy) means control of the senses in thought, word and deed.

(My Experiments with Truth; M.K. Gandhi)

No woman can be treated as the one having lost her honour unless she has consented for it. One who gets hurt in her attempt to protect her dignity from a rapist has her honour as a woman intact. . . . It shall be wrong to attach any kind of stigma with a woman who had been forcibly raped. The practice of hiding such ugly incidents from public knowledge must end. If society discusses openly about such problems appropriate solutions may be found.

(Harijan Sevak; 03.01.1942)

A woman who is attacked with intent of raping her should not think about merits or demerits of violence or non-violence. At that time her only duty would be to defend herself by any means. God has given her teeth, nails and strength; she must use them even if she has to die as a consequence.

Male or female, we all are afraid of death; hence we surrender. Some beg for mercy, some pay money to save them, some crawl like insects; similarly women may also feel helpless and stop struggling against animal behaviour of men. Fear of life makes a human being live like living corpse. Fighting against atrocious behavior of others is our Dharma. That is why I said women must fight fearlessly.

(Harijan Sevak; 03.01.1942)

I have said the woman is a symbol of sacrifice and non-violence. She has learned to protect her and her womanhood without depending on man.

(Harijan Sevak; 11.21.1936)

I do not differentiate between men and women. Women must feel as free as men. Courage is not a man's father's property. The art of self-protection does not depend on outside help.

(Harijan Sevak; 01.12.1947)

I have heavily relied on quotations from Gandhi's writings to discuss his views on woman. It is abundantly clear that Gandhi treated women as half of the human race who was as independent or dependent as men in all the matters of life. In Gandhi's opinion there was no question of viewing their status from the standpoint of theories and practices that have been evolved by male dominated societies and that have been in existence for over two thousand years.

Another issue that gets clarified is about Gandhi's perception of non-violence. Clear objective behind Gandhi's insistence on non-violence had been to demolish the thought of violence. He never thought of non-violence as an excuse for surrendering to a nonviolent action of someone who has lost his senses.

28

EDUCATION

An education which does not teach us to discriminate between good and bad, to assimilate the one and eschew the other, is a misnomer.

(Mahatma; D.G. Tendulkar)

Education should be so revolutionized as to answer the wants of the poorest villager, instead of answering those of an imperial exploiter.

(Mahatma; D.G. Tendulkar)

The first quote is about the education of a human being irrespective of time, space (say country) and circumstances. The second one is about the education of an Indian at the time of British rule in India. However, if we replace the word 'villager' by 'individual' and delete the word 'imperial' from the second quotation, it will become more generalized. Can we say that education today conforms to the stipulations made by Gandhi in above quotations? I think most of us would reply to this question in negative.

I give below a few more quotations from Gandhi to discuss the process of education.

> *Stuffing the mind with much information or passing examinations after reading various books is not true education. True education can be imparted only by building good character.*

(Mahatma Gandhi in England;
Mahadev Desai)

> *The thought that intellect can be developed only by gathering knowledge by reading many books is not the right thought. Learning physical skills that are productive (like that of a craftsman) through traditional methods is best for development of mind; this is the right thought.*

(Harijan Sevak; 01.16.1937)

> *In fact, true education begins only after leaving the school. The one who has understood it becomes a student forever. While performing his duty properly one gets ample opportunity to learn new things every day.*

(Satyagraha Ashram Ka Itihas; M.K.
Gandhi)

There is no doubt that best way to learn is experiencing. Man experiences most by using his mind, intellect and body together. In a good modern education system good educators are using this knowledge successfully. However, scant importance is being attached to character building. As a result awareness about the right duties and commitment for appropriate performance thereof is missing. There is growth, no doubt, but humanitarian values are being neglected.

What Gandhi said about seven to eight decades before was very relevant then. He was highly concerned about the children and youth of India because India's future after independence depended on them. Unfortunately, Gandhi's followers who took over the reins from him opted for a path that did not serve the country well. A country like China that was way behind India six to seven decades back and that adopted a route different from that of India after freedom, progressed better. China's leader Mao adopted three key thoughts; equality, self-dependence and total involvement of poor masses in Nation building. Mao was a Communist. Gandhi was for non-violence without any compromise. However, the three points adopted by Mao were in Gandhi's agenda also. Gandhi's path was not easy but it envisaged true and sustainable growth of individuals who were large in numbers (just as China had) and had inherent spiritual inclination of committing themselves to their Dharma (duty). Gandhi's thoughts might have helped India to have a very balanced growth, both physically and spiritually. This, however, needed sacrifice, patience and temperament of selfless service. Gandhi's followers who ruled India after its independence were impatient and overawed by the materialistic success of others oblivious to the roots thereof. They did not understand the essence and importance of self dependence.

> *Self dependence, for me, is not merely the foremost objective of basic education but it must be considered as the acid test for it . . . . Without the objective of self dependence the education may be viewed as a body without life.*

> *When you teach a person that he could produce, with his own efforts, clothes to avoid going naked, in itself is an education.*

(Harijan Sevak; 08.25.1946)

> *Right type of intellectual development is possible only through productive use of physical labour. Intellectual development is possible even otherwise, but in that case there is no guarantee of the nature of its outcome. Right development includes all the three kinds of developments; intellectual, physical and spiritual.*

(Harijan Sevak; 09.22.1946)

Without the right temperament of being useful for others, intellectual growth remains one sided. Serving others selflessly and being useful for others are spiritual tendencies. This is the region of 'Atma' (soul or spirit). Intellectual growth must be synchronized with spiritual and physical growth.

(Harijan Sevak; 04.17.1937)

It can be easily understood that Gandhi viewed education as means for knowing the art and science of living with others and putting the knowledge gained into practice. It is learning to make right use of the faculties of body, mind, intellect and ego (I am-ness) granted by the nature (the Almighty God) for survival of human beings in society. Three important components of education according to Gandhi are; knowledge (both physical and spiritual) that has been internalized and practiced; total self-sufficiency and self-dependence with one's own physical and mental efforts and; spirit of selfless service and the natural urge to be useful for others. Gandhi, in a way, thought of merging individual ego of man with those whom he served selflessly.

As such Gandhi's concepts on learning cover a very vast area of human life; and it had to be so because he was basically a very honest experimenter who had the knack of entering into billions and billions of minds of human beings who ever lived on this earth; to educate himself, that is, to explore the truth. A few more aspects deserve a place in this chapter. One such aspect is about the basic temperament that a student must possess.

Persistent questioning and healthy inquisitiveness are foremost requisites for acquiring knowledge of any kind.

**(The Mind of Mahatma Gandhi;
Editors, Prabhu and Rao)**

A seeker must seek minimum logical answers to his questions on the issues he has faith (shraddha) in. He should never be insistent on getting his imaginary doubt resolved. If any step is to be taken then some inquiries may be raised about the likely merits and demerits of the steps. If some clarification has to be sought about some incident the incident must be narrated with honesty and in detail. Such questions must not be made public because then there are great chances of the issue landing in the realm of utter confusion and the basic issue having been totally lost.

**(The Diary of Mahadev Desai;
Editor, N.D. Parikh))**

The above two statements from Gandhi do not contradict each other. The first is about ordinary matters of life. A problem of mathematics, a law of science or an issue of economics must be understood fully. How different knots are tied and when to be tied depending upon the application must be learned thoroughly and practiced. However, if one is not able to convince himself beyond a point as to how touching feet of elders with utmost respect is beneficial; it is better to continue to touch feet of elders if it is an satisfying experience, even without being convince of the logic behind it. If a child believes that he can go to Mount Everest sitting on the shoulder of his father who is lame, let him live with this belief till he holds that faith. Faith that makes one fearless and helps him to think of positive things that do not cause any harm need not become an issue of concern in our life. The outcome of such faith can not cause any harm. It has been observed that some people are in a habit of making issues of even harmless faith subjects of much intellectual argumentation. This does not serve any purpose. It confuses them as well as others.

Gandhi conceptualized *the universe* for an individual, as a manageable field that he can serve selflessly without insurmountable problems. Such field alone could become his immediate surroundings. Obviously, one's education must also be related to his immediate surroundings.

> *The way we have discarded British rule*
> *that was forced upon us; we must discard*
> *their language that suppressed our*

culture. There is no doubt that English shall continue to occupy its position as an international language for international politics and trade.

(Harijan Sevak; 09.25.1947)

Just as we do not want that others should exploit us we also should not think of exploiting others . . . . We want our children to become productive to bring about fundamental changes in our country to restructure our society.

(Harijan Sevak; 02.12.1938)

I am not emphasizing upon industry and trade; my emphasis is on handicrafts and knowledge of literature, history, geography, mathematics, science and other such subjects.

My views on the process of education are based on the idea of teaching subjects by relating them to their practical aspects and uses. For example, take the art of spinning; that can be taught along with imparting knowledge about varieties of cotton grown, the regions of India where cotton is grown, the type of land suitable for cultivation etc.. With spinning students can also be taught the history of how the traditional textile industry was destroyed and what the political reasons behind it were. History of British Empire can also be included in such teaching. Calculating and mathematics would also appear likewise.

We have to make our children true representatives of our strong culture and civilization. The basic education must make them self dependent.

(Harijan Sevak; 10.30.1937)

I am not against high education, but I am definitely against the kind of high education that is being provided in my country. In my scheme of things there shall be best of libraries and laboratories. We must have a big army of engineers, chemists, experts in different subjects and sectors of knowledge. They should all be true servants of their nation and its people; who should strive to become more and more aware of their rights and necessities. These men of knowledge must speak the language of the people of India and not that of a foreign country. The knowledge they gain must be the joint property of the people of India. When this happens some genuine and creative work shall be done by India instead of generating only fake by copying others. Of course, the cost of this education shall be equitably borne by the people of this country in a justified manner.

(Harijan Sevak; 07.09.1938)

I really feel very sad to state that Gandhi's followers who ruled India after its independence did just the opposite of what Gandhi proposed. They established such educational institutes and commissioned such educational systems at very high costs incurred by people of India; that the knowledge capital built by those institutes and systems was not of much use for India itself; instead it helped the rich foreign countries to make more profits and gains for them. Gandhi's thought that true independence comes from self-dependence was buried by those whose minds could not adopt the thought of freedom.

Neither the universe is different from us nor are we different from the universe. One influences the other. Thought itself is a work or action. No thought is ever wasted. We must practice to generate good thoughts and generating good thoughts must be made a habit.

(The Diary of Mahadev Desai; Editor, N.D. Parikh)

29

DRISHYATE ANEN ITI DARSHANAM

The process through which one is able to view the truth is **Darshan.** This is the meaning of the heading of this chapter. Ancient Indian scriptures used the word *darshan* for what we generally understand when we use the English word *philosophy.*

Considerable importance is given to 'problem solving' in modern science education. Good teachers advise their students to understand the problem full well before attempting to solve them because only about 15% students are able to grasp the importance of viewing the problem correctly before attempting to solve it. Learning this technique is relatively easy because the problems do not change during the time period it is being solved. However, modern student knows that in this competitive world, when he appears for a competitive examination, restrictions of time land him into a strange situation. If he is able to understand the problem correctly the correct way of solving it may not occur to him or a particular way of solving problem may prejudice him to view the problem incorrectly.

Now, let us imagine a situation when the problems before us are changing and we, as the solvers of the problems, are also changing due to onslaught of information that we are forced to gather. The situation becomes more complicated by the inertia of physical world that also includes inertia of our own intellect (for example, prejudices that we suffer from due to our own previous learning). Can we say, with fair degree of confidence that we are good at handling our own life and the life of entire human race of today and that of tomorrow? This question cannot be easily answered in affirmative.

To me it appears that the human race has divided itself into three categories. The first consists of people who are trying to survive somehow till they die. They have surrendered themselves to their pains and sorrows. The second type has completely surrendered them to their own bodies and desires. They are busy with overcoming their pains and sorrows by developing more and more desires, with no success. The third type, I would prefer to call them modern intelligentsia, are the people living in their drawing rooms with vacuum cleaners to suck all types of thoughts that do not conform to their prejudices to be subsequently dumped into dustbins. Then they scrutinize what remains to find what can be sold at a price through which they can afford to buy luxuries, comforts or at least some recognition. To become convinced of the thoughts that sell is the **pravritti** of modern intelligentsia.

Many of the readers must have noticed that the above classification is influenced by the thoughts of Marx, Lenin and other communist thinkers. Gandhi, Marx, Mao or Lenin, I cannot doubt the purity of their intentions. Communism has been tried. Russian revolution failed. It did not consider the farmers. China took care of mainly farmers. It succeeded in bringing about some changes but the main architect responsible for those changes was forgotten. It is now playing the same game that west is playing, of course on its own terms. It is not my job to make predictions, the only thing I have to say is that Gandhi had been closest to truth but historical realties and his own body did not give him the time he needed.

Behind everything, even spirituality, there is man. God does not need man; the man needs God. Man can not invent tools to conquer nature. He has physical limitations; his body, his mind, his intellect and his ego are imperfect. He cannot ensure eternal happiness by making use of the physical tools he possesses (of body, mind, intellect and ego) if he deploys them only for his personal use. Because, if everyone in the world does that the world will become a surrounding that is hostile to the individuals living therein. However, man has the ability to realize the universal consciousness through his faith in God. This consciousness can make this planet a place worth living. There is no need to doubt what I have said in this paragraph. An infant who has no ability to protect himself has two protectors in this world; the God and his mother. The God acts through human beings other than the child's mother who are kind. Even if thirty percent of human beings learn to take half the care of their immediate surroundings that a mother takes of her small child; the history of human race will change.

Death in a violent encounter is more real than imagined wound in a non-violent struggle, if human beings get united. It is strange to see that mankind prefer to die after numerous suicidal surrenders to the violence of others than to an imaginary wound in a non-violent protest. God made arrangements for food, cloth and shelter for all the human beings that are born. He gave us similar mental and physical abilities. If many of us are underfed, half naked, without proper shelter and are discriminated on the basis of colour of skin, class, caste, race, gender or education, the God cannot be held responsible for it. Those, who circulated philosophies based on violent thoughts and conditioned our minds through their persistent efforts; are to be blamed. Those, who tell us the world created by the God would remain as violent as ever and nothing can be done about it because it is an illusion; are to be blamed. We, who due to our ignorance, fear or due to our selfish designs do not try to find the truth, instead keep on passing the buck in all directions; are to be blamed.

How can we expect a blind man to describe a scenario? Similarly how can we expect people who are blinded by violent or escapist philosophies or **darshan** to have a view on non-violence?

Considerable introspection and unlearning is needed to understand Gandhi.

The explosion in communication technology has greatly influenced thinking process of human mind. 'How to view' i.e. the process of **darshan** is a mental process. Mind needs peace and aloneness through detachment to view the truth in things properly. Just as electromagnetic waves have energy and momentum, thoughts also have energy and momentum. Huge availability of information for which scientists, technocrats and Information Technology sector is taking much credit is ruining human capacity to view things independently and making genuine inquiries. Thinking about the physical world and materialistic life and making use of it is in order and is also needed. Having born on this earth we have no other option but to think about physical life of the mankind and we must do it. We must do it with a view to organizing our worldly affairs so that we develop urge and give enough time for our spiritual development. It is very unfortunate that many spiritualists, even the very renowned ones from my own country, are trying to put the cart before the horse. The need is for managing our worldly affairs to make spiritual gains; and not for managing our spiritual affairs for materialistic gains. It can easily be imagined that when the modern spiritualists themselves are completely out of focus then what must be happening to those who are centered on materialistic gains only, by choice or by compulsion. Selfish intentions and faulty viewing are minimizing our concern for the universe (we may call it our immediate surroundings), permitting it to become a sham and loading all our efforts for the welfare of mankind with intelligence that is flawed.

The thoughts or philosophies with superficial variations that are gaining momentum today are essentially violent in nature. They are violent because they are not selfless, they are not humble, they are discriminating and they are ridden with the feeling of doer—ship. Their momentum is increasing day by day because more and more people are getting influenced by such thoughts and philosophies.

Our problem is that we are slaves of our **pravrittis** and our prejudices. When we read and listen to the word 'violence' our mind thinks of physical violence only.

Physical violence is just a form of violence. If a father slaps his son on finding him telling a lie, perhaps he is not violent; but when he helps him by arranging a fake medical certificate for his unjustified absence in his school, he is definitely violent towards his child, by showing him the way as to how to manage one's unjustified acts.

Similarly, if I knowingly insert a few things in this book that are not true, to ensure that more people read it; I shall not be non-violent as that may cause some harm to someone.

Yet another thing I wish to add here is that Gandhi was a human being. He was not God. He was deeply hurt in his last days when India was suffering due to communal violence during partition of India and when he found that his followers were making basic mistakes of adopting politics of ruling instead of politics of service. Physically weak as he was, he perhaps became aware that he could not turn the tide towards greater truth; he then preferred to err on the safer side in the larger interests of humanity.

Today, I feel I have no followers. If there were any, such ugly incidents (the communal riots) could not have taken place.

(Harijan Sevak; 04.20.1947)

The life of crores, is my politics. I have no courage to leave it, as that would mean negating all efforts of my life and also existence of God.

(Harijan Sevak; 08.17.1947)

The ideal thing for me at this stage should be, having no desire to live for 125 years and at the same time; not having desire to die looking at the adverse circumstance of today.

(Speech in New Delhi; 10.05.1947)

There is no logic in evaluating Gandhi on the basis of historical realities that he had to face in his last days. Honesty demands that I evaluate my own statement whereby I have said that Gandhi erred on the safer side at the time of partition of India. I have said it on the basis of my understanding that partition did not benefit the people of either of the countries. The question is whether I have a mind that is more non-violent than that of the mind of Gandhi? I admit that I have a mind, much more violent than many, what to speak of Gandhi's. Still I made that statement to highlight a point that no philosophy should be judged on the basis of **pravritti** and prejudices of the one who tries to judge them. The matter does not end here. I cannot even say with confidence that partition of India had been bad both for India and Pakistan. Who knows, maybe it was for the better.

Notwithstanding the above, I submit that either the spirituality appears to have a few inconsistencies sometimes or finding consistency in spirituality is beyond us. As against this the material world has many inconsistencies most of the time. While dealing with worldly affairs we often encounter unpleasant situations that do not leave any scope of making a right choice. The one who is sufficiently detached knows how to err on the safer side. I suspect even the God gets it done through human beings. This I write not with intentions of glorifying or defending Gandhi; he needs neither, nor am I competent to do any such thing. Hence, here is one more lesson we learn from Gandhi; of erring on the safer side when in dilemma.

I devoted this chapter to the question of how to view things and also to express my strong apprehensions about how making of genuine fundamental inquiries by ordinary people is becoming rarer day to day.

The title of the last chapter I have copied from Gandhi's vastly read book, *My Experiments with Truth*; it is *Farewell.*

30

FAREWELL

Let us say non-violence means causing no harm.

Are our governments non-violent? Are our industries, economic policies, trade & commerce, advertising etc. non-violent? Are our education systems non violent? Is our media non-violent? Are our cultures and religions non-violent? Are the organizations we work with to earn our livelihood non-violent? Are our hospitals and doctors non-violent? Is the man next door non-violent? Am I non-violent?

I fail to understand why there does not exist a direct word for 'non-violence'? We do not use 'non-hate' for love. Neither in Sanskrit nor in English we have a direct word for non-violence? We put 'non' before 'violence' or put '**A**' (negation) before '**himsa**' (violence) to call it **ahimsa**.

Human beings, by nature, want less miseries and more happiness. Animals with less intelligence instinctively search for food. The man, the intelligent one, thinks about growing food. His mind is never at rest. He thinks about what he sees and also tries to think beyond it.

Animals know only that much their creator has permitted them to know. I can express this in two ways; either I can say that animal is a part of nature or I can say animal is a slave of nature. Animal does not 'think' about nature. It accepts it or it has been made to accept it. The case of man is different because he can think. He may consider himself as part of the nature; let us say, then he has a kind of 'part—consciousness' that makes him think that he is a part of nature. He may also think of nature as a tyrant ruler who dictates all the terms in one's life; in that case man may feel that he is a slave of nature and develops 'slave-consciousness'. Perhaps, those with 'slave-consciousness' did not want to remain as a slave when they decided to conquer the nature. The word *pravritti* implies natural response of human beings to deal with the external world for his survival making use of all that he possesses viz. his body, mind, intellect, senses, sensory desires and ego.

Here, my intention is to discuss something about man's response to the external world.

A mother does many things to her very small child with intention to protect and take care of his body, like cleaning, massaging etc. Most of it is not liked by the child. He cries to express his anger but he does not abandon his 'part—consciousness' and clings to his mother at the very first opportunity. Animal and a small child have small needs, food and if possible some security. They both are dependent; animal on nature and a small human child on his mother. Case of grown up human beings is different. He can do many things for his survival and for reducing his miseries. He becomes fully aware of his dependence on the nature and his own intelligence that can help him to survive with lesser difficulties. First he wants freedom from hunger. And then starts his long journey with a clear motive of not remaining just a slave of the external world. Some who are able to view things correctly realize that throughout their lives they would have no option but to depend on the external world. There is no freedom from it. They, then, try to make themselves free of 'slave—consciousness' and adopt 'part—consciousness' to attain peace. They consider them as part of this nature and the universe.

The others continue to think about themselves as slaves of nature and hence live as slaves of the external world. They become the slaves of their *pravrittis*. They want to conquer the nature, with all the animate and inanimate that exists therein, hoping to attain freedom from their slavery. They harm nature, they harm fellow human beings, and they harm whatever they can harm if it helps them to satisfy their physical and mental needs and their desires. They enlarge their external world with things and objects that can make them more secure, more assured; they look for objects that give them more comforts to minimize their physical inconveniences or look for ways to derive more pleasure from their lives to reduce mental miseries; unaware of the fact that in this process they become more attached to their 'slave-consciousness'. Their faculties of body, mind, senses, sensory desires, intellect and ego become completely oriented towards the external world and take the man under their control. The man becomes a slave of himself. This is an excited state; whose outcome is violence. The one who is violent is not violent selectively. He is violent towards everything and everybody, including himself.

Let us accept this fact that most of us are violent. That is why we are stressed, distressed, unsatisfied, frustrated, depressed and sad or carry such emotions that cannot be termed as positive. When we are in this state, we are miserable and also become a cause of miseries for others. We may not act violently in physical sense but we knowingly or unknowingly cause harm. We cause harm to self and we also cause harm to our surroundings.

One who considers him as part of this nature or this universe views things differently. First, he realizes his limitations. He comes to know that his body, mind, senses and intellect have limitations. Then, some of those who have realized human limitations may try to understand the natural laws and their intent. If they fail to find an answer through external world (that has always happened in the history of mankind so far) they may not give up. They may continue, minimizing all that distracts their intellects and empowering their faith that they would get the answer one day to attain peace of mind. They are more likely to be satisfied that they are making right efforts in their lives. In addition to this, if they possess compassion for others they live with, they may also try to include them in their efforts. If they do all this, they lovingly and peacefully, transform their 'part—consciousness' into 'participant—consciousness'.

To summarize, man after realizing his inadequacies and helplessness can have three types of consciousnesses. First, to beg, steal, borrow or fight to ensure his victory over the external world. Second is to accept supremacy of external world; and to explore universal laws to find ways to attain peace and happiness for his individual self. The third is to include fellow being in his efforts to explore universal laws to attain peace and happiness for all so that life becomes a pleasant journey not for him alone but for all.

I will take a small pause here to say that perhaps, Gandhi had attained an advanced state of 'participant-consciousness' and had attained a kind of *Moksha* much before his death. For all one knows, his physical death might have been merely a worldly affair for the world to worry about. *Moksha* means total freedom from fear.

In ideal non-violence you refuse to accept the duality of master-slave, offence-defense, material-spiritual, gain-loss, and victory-defeat; you get rid of all temptations and fear and make others realize that we all are participants of this infinite and ageless universe.

In my opinion those who try to create confusions about what is ideal and what is practical; negate both. They say what should not be done can be done and what should be done they cannot do. They are simply superstitious people having no scientific temperament. Science demands that a fact is something that has been verified experimentally and has a sound theoretical basis. Experiments do not perfectly match the theory due to physical constraints;

they, however, very closely and consistently approximate the theory and provide workable knowledge. The correct thought is keeping the ideal before ourselves and striving to achieve it. That is being practical. The utterances of those who reject the theory itself because it cannot be fully realized are not worth anything and do not deserve any attention.

We have seen that the thought of violence can not arise if we consider ourselves as a part of universe just as all living beings are. We can replace the word universe by nature (*prakriti*) or *the infinite whole*. No doubt, we are governed by certain laws that we can only party understand. They are the laws of God; but because we cannot directly interact with God due to our own limitations we may call them universal laws. All that exists in the nature differs from one another but everything has its purpose in the functioning of universe. Lions kill other animals to satisfy their hunger. It regulates population of some weaker animals by eating them, lest the weaker animals eat away all vegetation. I have heard arguments that human violence regulates human population. I reject them because such arguments place man at par with animals. Man has intelligence that is why he has *purushartha*. Man alone can make efforts to free himself of the cycles of birth and death, according to ancient Indian philosophy. Man alone has the ability to conduct himself according to his choice.

A lion does not know the purpose of its existence. It also does not know how to satisfy its desires through violence.

If lions start using their strength, teeth and nails to kill others just for the fun of it, nature's balance shall get disturbed. Lion kill to feed them and to protect them; and for no other purpose. They have no desires. They have instincts. Man has intelligence that no other living being has. He can decide when to regulate his population and how to do it. He is freer than others to decide and act. He has thought deeply and defined his Dharma to live a better life so that all live a reasonably happy and purposeful life. Man has also found that any life only for the purposes of satisfying one's materialistic desires does not reduce miseries; on the contrary it enhances them, for him and also for others. In the history of mankind, it has not been made possible till date that majority of human beings have lived lives of physical comfort and only a few found it difficult to survive. It had always been just the opposite of it. If majority of people are still living an inferior life than fellow human beings, it is enough of an indication that growth of humanity had not been proper.

If human intellect is worth anything then the least one should expect from it is to ensure that the entire humanity lives without worries for his food, clothes, shelter, health and security. Neither going to Mars for detailed investigation of that planet nor attaining *Mokshas* are indications of superiority of human intellect. The intellect human beings possess is a very fine tool that no other living being possesses. The fault is with us. We are not able to adjust this precious tool of ours to keep it in proper alignment with our spiritual existence and materialistic existence. In simple and scientific language our intellect is not aligned to universal laws.

The world has been developing in a strange way. Gandhi's popularity in India after his death depended on his pictures printed on currency notes and the films made on or about him. The articles I read on Gandhi try to say, "Gandhi is still relevant today." Children are taught that Gandhi gave us freedom. Management Schools are teaching thoughts of Gandhi after extracting its essence and throwing it away.

What Gandhi said might not have been that relevant when the Mahabhart (war) was fought. Gandhi might not have been relevant when Vishnu Gupta Chanakya decided to dethrone and ultimately dethroned incompetent king Dhanananda, to establish a powerful kingdom that was just to its people. Gandhi might not have been necessary to free India from British rule. But Gandhi became very relevant for India from the day British left India. Gandhi is becoming increasing relevant for the entire world now. If we continue viewing our lives the way we do it today, he would become extremely relevant for future generations.

I am fully aware that when small people make big statements no one cares. I am also aware that if I strongly feel about something, then expressing it is my Dharma. And, if I follow my Dharma it matters to me (an entity that tends to zero); because a zero with all its humility placed under the smallest possible number results into infinity. Being at the last chapter of the book I have started learning a few things from Gandhi.

Many consider that solutions offered by Gandhi to the problems in the world cannot give desired results; but no one appears to have questioned Gandhi's assessments of the problems the world faced. The simple way in which he applied his common sense in analyzing the problems of his time baffled the smartest of the people in his time. We all have common sense but for some reason or the other become subdued in expressing what we feel and experience. Are we good at assessing what is going on in our surroundings?

According to what I observe today, I grade our intellectual efforts in order of their superiority as follows. At the lowest rung is *common sense*; because we do not trust our senses. Perhaps we are aware that we have no control on our senses. Then, there is *wisdom*, that we use sparingly as it often relates to the process, not the result, and we take pride in calling ourselves 'result-oriented'. Next in the ladder is *knowledge*. Traditionally knowledge is important because we cannot do things without the required knowledge. At the top rung is *information*. To properly understand why information is at the top, not knowledge, let us think about the age old practice of use of spies. Modern man is always in a war situation. Today who is interested in excellence? To win, it is enough to be a mediocre with the right information and the 'right desire' to serve oneself. What if one has invented something that improves living standards of those who are very poor, if the available information suggests that it cannot be profitably marketed? I am sure many of my readers who might have had the personal experience of this phenomenon would understand fully what I am trying to communicate. Our intellect is being guided by the desires we have and the information we have about the external world. If this kind of ladder is being used to put in intellectual efforts by about one tenth of world's population, who influences world opinion, then, I must say the violence is settling deeper in human life. Are we not becoming so self-centered that we even mould the facts according to our interests and conveniences? If one tenth of people misguide nine tenth of world population, it is nothing but violence.

As long as we live, material is a reality for us. If man considers his physical life as illusion he may be making a mistake. But what if he considers his physical existence as the only reality? And what if the material has a desire to exist? And what if material has the intelligence and ability to manipulate its surroundings? Then, our 'common sense' tells us that unless each material particle has a strong desire and commitment to co-exist with other particles, the physical world shall collapse. Desire to exist with no concern for one's surrounding is violence. Desire to co-exist with others is non-violence.

Treating the life as purely materialistic is very dangerous. The problem aggravates when each material particle desires to realize its 'true materialistic growth potential' and begins its efforts to grow into a mountain. If this becomes an ideal to achieve and a 'common sense' for all, man loses all control.

The common sense does not work unless it is selfless. To be able to live in peace, we, then have no other option but to turn to the selfless and the wise, the creators of the scriptures. Scriptures exist for the man. In Lincoln's language; they are by the man, of the man and for the man. It shall be relevant to quote a section of *Nasadiya Sukta* from *Rigveda.*

Iyam Visrishtiryat. Aababhoova yadi va dadhe yadi va na.
Yo. Aasyadhyakshah parame vyomantso aanga ved yadi va na ved.

[Meaning: What is the origin of this creation? This may be answered by the one who has created it, if He has (actually) created it. Or it can be answered by one who has watched it being originated, from the highest of heavens, or maybe even He does not know it.]

There is no imagination, no myth and no prejudice. The Sukta doubts if someone has created this universe. This is a case of spirituality evolving from purely materialistic considerations. That spirituality is only about the unseen and the unknown is a myth.

Some may argue that how is it possible that thoughts of scriptures could be made applicable in modern times when scriptures were created thousands of years ago? The answer to this question is that man was the point of consideration in scriptures not the time. The background used in scriptures might have been ancient but the philosophical essence is unlikely to vary with time. Moreover ancient Indian scriptures have prescribed that Dharma can vary according to place time and circumstances. It means those who are learned, wise, selfless and deeply concerned about humanity; and have spotless character and are *sthitprajna;* can contemplate and decide if some provisions of Dharma need some revision. They must consult their contemporaries and very carefully think if proposed revisions do not cause any harm to nature and humanity and are according to truth. Such revisions make scriptures more powerful. If Gandhi thought that politics should be based on truth and non-violence he was absolutely right. Political intellect should also be aligned to universal consciousness; after all politics is also for man and man alone.

The problem we face in modern times is that those who influence the masses in all walks of life are generally violent and selfish. Even the best among them are misguided about spirituality, religion, right human conduct and all the qualities that we have covered in this book treating them as essential for a **sadhak**. Modern thinkers are feeding human mind with thoughts that they classify as realistic (materialistic) or religious (or spiritual).Those who are believed to be having realistic thoughts accept the world on 'as is where is' basis and call it real world. The improvements they think of are either mere patchworks or extrinsic in nature without taking into account *pravrittis* of human beings. Many realists, who intend well for man, make use of human *pravrittis* to set the things right but to no avail. Yes, I am hinting at those who think of human welfare through violent revolutions and at also those who recommend free market economies for a world they accept on 'as is where is' basis. Serious thinkers with religious orientation suggest 'cleaning' of man without bothering about the 'polluting reality' that surrounds him.

Modern man, in general, does not have to worry about ferocious animal, floods, landslides, storms or while in search of his food becoming a food himself of other creatures. Modern man has to struggle against his own society for his survival. This struggle for his survival continues; either due to his excessive desires or due to his unfulfilled basic needs; either against physical violence or mental violence. In this struggle either he is an oppressor or one who has consented to surrender. Man is not free.

Live and let others live; this is our Dharma. We are neither living the way we should be living nor are we permitting others to live as a free human being by virtue of being a participant in the system that has brought the entire humanity to this predicament.

Poor living standards of life for many, discrimination, hatred, violence, cruelty etc. are pains that humanity suffer from. They are pains, the symptoms of the disease we suffer from. We try to treat symptoms without trying to diagnose the root cause of disease. Some try to suggest how to compete and succeed to become a part and parcel of a unreasonably selfish class who corner maximum possible wealth for itself by depriving others; some offer modern or ancient remedies for getting relief from stresses generated due to modern competitive life styles; some work hard to empower those who have been deprived by the selfish class of what was rightfully theirs, to ensure that they are able to pull themselves out of their poverty and some extend charities to feel good about their benevolence. Nations buy more arms to maintain peace. We treat everything as some commodity. We invent to sell. We create new markets. We sell disease and then also sell the pain killers to reduce pain caused by the disease. We are so busy in glorifying ourselves by deploying our intelligence and taking risks to add high values to our materialistic achievements that we have become totally oblivious to the fact that the tumour we have implanted in human society is enlarging every day and the burden thereof shall have to be borne by our future generations. I pity the intellect of those who say life is an illusion and pity the intellect of those also who sell *mantars* for success in life. I call it intellectual bankruptcy.

Earlier violence was killing human beings. Today violence is systematically dehumanizing the human society. The most critical thing is that oppressors have been successful in selling the thought of violence to the oppressed also.

The happenings of today and where they are leading us to; do not permit us to believe that we are a non-violent society. We cannot even say with confidence that we, individually or collectively, are making enough efforts to convert it into a non-violent society. Gandhi did not write or say the lines given below but he always appeared to mean them.

God takes care of human beings. Having faith in God is meaningless unless we human beings do not take care of humanity. And humanity can be taken care of only through Ahimsa.

Violence can be sold easily because it can be packaged very attractively. It can be made to look gorgeous, sophisticated, elegant and towering. It appeals to our senses but only till our eyes are directed towards it. Anything to look good or give pleasure to our senses, unless it is freely available in the nature, has to be structured by collecting material from this earth. It does not generate anything to support our existence. It does not replenish the material it has drawn to beautify itself. The science of violence is to deprive the universal body for providing sensory pleasure to a few. The thought of satisfying one's senses by eating up from one's own body is violence. The question is not that much about who owns what; the question is of how the resources of planet earth are being utilized. Human life is not going to end after hundred years. In our effort to provide food to a much bigger population than that of hundred year's back, thanks to our intellect that enhanced productivity of our modern tools, we have also wasted a bigger proportion of the resources to provide for comfort and lavish life styles of increasing number of people. The end result had been the ever increasing gap between those who have and those who do not have. God provided enough so that all can happily live. Are we sure we are not playing a game of consuming more and more and replenishing less and less to nature? No one questions the superiority of human mind, but do we have a picture of earth five hundred year ago and a projected picture of our planet of five hundred years hence? We are not increasing our material wealth; we are increasing our unproductive material wealth. Nature gave us enough to maintain our body, mind, intellect and senses in healthy and happy state. Less physical efforts to fulfill ones needs, more comforts, ostentatious life styles, greater desires for sensory pleasures and going after excessive conveniences cannot be achieved without using natural resources. Once these resources are drawn they no longer become available to us after recycling. Not only this, there are consumption patterns that cause immediate harm to nature. For example, petrol once burnt not only depletes the resources but also cause pollution. Larger the gap between our actual needs as human beings and our consumption, graver shall be the consequences of violence caused by us. The harmful consequences of environmental imbalances and pollution will be many times greater for our future generation than what they are for present generations. Simplicity and restraint are not the qualities that are needed by spiritual and saintly persons alone; they are needed by all.

Some may argue that I have widened the net of violence and am trying to trap almost all in it. I would say that modern man has not restrained himself in excessively deploying his intelligence for satisfying his sensory desires and have fallen in a trap that he cannot escape from. First there is no easy escape route. Second, he does not have the will to come out of it. I do not think that modern man is not aware of his violence. It seems he has become helpless in dealing with his desires. He is fearful that if he tried to exercise restraint he will get into a bigger rut. Those who are deriving maximum benefit from this state of affairs have resorted to manipulating things through misleading statistics, propaganda, advertising, lobbying, showcasing and, of course, complicating issues, that expose the harm being caused, to levels where only confusion prevails.

In this chapter I have tried to discuss about the continuation of violent **pravritti** of human being that was passed on from generation to generation. Earlier in some regions it had been in control due to intervention of the wise and learned, in others it was not. History of invasions and wars by those with violent minds virtually destroyed the thought of **Dharma**. This is my personal opinion that **ethics** have 'healthy survival of the society' as its objective, whereas **Dharma** has 'healthy survival of the universal man' as its objective.

Gandhi, at a particular juncture, appeared in this world and seeded the thought of fundamental change in the world. I have tried my level best to keep the soul of Gandhi's thoughts intact in this book by not permitting any outside thoughts, except those from scriptures, to enter in this book. So far in this book I took up different elements and tried to describe them so that they grow into small thoughts; now I shall endeavour to integrate them to present what Gandhi stood for. I do this as a student, not as an expert. I have preferred to use separate paragraphs for different streams of thoughts. I have avoided using subtitles to allow a natural flow.

NEED FOR INTERNAL REVOLUTION

It is difficult to say whether many practical truths that serve the universe well get unified to become absolute truth or it is other way round. This, however, is certain that source of all truths is universal intelligence that has God's blessings and not human intelligence. Man's *Dharma* is to explore the truth, internalize it and follow it. The one who does not leave truth whatever may be the consequences becomes an example and others should try to learn from him.

Truth is our basis, our goal and our ideal all the time. If we leave it we become dangerous for the universe, for others and also for ourselves. Truth is the supreme thought. It is the ultimate reference, from where we begin and at which we terminate. It is our **sadhya**.

Non-violence (*Ahimsa*) is a conduct. It stipulates that one should not cause any harm to others of any kind, that is, physical, mental or through words. It is the surest tool to help us realize the truth. It is **sadhan** to achieve the **sadhya**. In fact, universal intelligence demands that all living beings live for doing good to the universe or in other words to serve the universe appropriately. Living beings other than human beings have been created with inherent intelligence to serve nature. They have no choice.

Man has his own intelligence. He is free to think and act subject to his limitations. He has a wavering mind that gets influenced by the external world and his desires to satisfy and please his senses. It remains always doubtful whether and to what extent he would do well for the universe. The wise and the learned of high moral values have, therefore, prescribed that man, at least, should not cause any harm to anybody, directly or indirectly. That is the essence of non-violence.

> *Ahimsa and truth are so intertwined that it is practically impossible to disentangle and separate them.*

(Truth is God; R.K. Prabhu)

In the above quote Gandhi intended to express that when **sadhan** becomes necessary and sufficient to realize **sadhya**, **sadhan** itself becomes **sadhya**.

Gandhi had the rare selflessness, simplicity and courage to call spades a spade. I have no intention to undermine many other great thinkers who understood things as clearly as Gandhi. In fact Gandhi learned from many of them. Gandhi is found a step ahead of others because of his experiments with the basics and drawing the essence of non-violence from ancient Indian scriptures.

While Gandhi agrees and accepts, in principle, that purpose of human life is to achieve freedom from the cycles of births and deaths, that is to attain *Moksha* through realization of truth (for him truth itself was God); he considers that serving humanity to reduce its pains and sorrows should be the first priority for a human being. He believed that serving humanity was a sacred duty that must be selflessly performed to realize a practical truth (or immediate truth). All what he did throughout his life, whether in India or South Africa was to serve humanity.

What distinguishes Gandhi from perhaps, all others is the way he went about doing what he did. He started, executed and completed his jobs with utmost humility and **shraddha** (devotion, commitment, faith, love, care and attention). He studied and contemplated, stayed closer to the deprived sections, worked like them, led an austere life and did physical labour. He reviewed the tasks he accomplished and extracted all that was there to learn from them. For him methods were more important than the results; means were more important than the ends. He worked on himself to get rid of his own shortcomings and weaknesses. He took each task as an experiment and completed it strictly keeping the truth as his ideal and non-violence as his uncompromising code of conduct. He kept no secrets. The world could easily become aware of successes, failures or shortfalls of his experiments. The purpose of this book is not to discuss about his lifestyle or the sacrifices he made to serve people. I have briefly narrated only a very few things about him, only to emphasize that behind his thoughts was the strength of his personal experiences and experimentations, that he carried out diligently. There was no difference between his deeds and words.

Gandhi's concept and accepted process for effecting revolutionary changes in social, political, economic and all other systems was pivoted on transforming the man and empowering him to become self-dependent in tackling his own problem. He did not believe in charity and he thought that an ideal democracy means having minimal governance. His dream was that people live together helping each other, taking care of each other and causing no harm to any living being. For most of us this is unachievable. I remember to have read somewhere that Albert Einstein once said, "If the facts don't fit the theory change the facts." This statement of Einstein makes my job of explaining a subtle point of my understanding about Gandhi relatively simple.

According to ancient Indian scriptures we all, in our true form are parts of the Supreme soul, anxiously waiting for our merger with Him. That is our true nature (*swabhav*). It is only due to our current form as human beings we think and act differently. God is flawless, and so we nearly are; if and when we realize our true nature. If all of us are parts of that INFINITE ONE, there is no duality, no contradiction, no two interests and no two aspirations. If the facts about human being and humanity do not fit into the theory given in our scriptures, we should try changing the man. Is it possible? Gandhi thought that it was, provided one acquired the right intelligence and made right efforts with devotion. When I am using the word scriptures, I am referring to ancient Indian philosophy (*darshan*) that is believed to have a logical and scientific base. I am not referring to mythological stories and mysticism. We move on to discuss what are right intelligence and right efforts.

Gandhi believed that only the God was perfect. He often said that God does not make mistakes. He was aware of human limitations also. He accepted that human beings cannot fully understand God and how He acted to get something accomplished. In his opinion the only thing man can do is to build understanding of divine laws. For example, Gandhi had full faith that non-violence was a divine law. But, whether it is law or an accepted principle subject to some conditions is not known to us. Our authority as human beings is limited to making selfless efforts for serving the humanity and deeply contemplating about divine laws; but getting the fruits of our efforts and knowing the absolute truth are beyond us. Let us understand it with an example. If we make efforts, without any self interest, without causing any harm and without any ego, to convert a violent person into a non-violent one; having faith in God and his decision and pray devotedly for his consent and help; we may succeed. However, we must remember, that will only be the kindness of God, not our doing. We have a right to act selflessly but we have no right on the outcome or fruits of our efforts. The right effort means an effort for a right cause where fruits of the efforts are surrendered to the God; and right intelligence means the one which is according to universal intelligence. Universal intelligence necessitates that the outcome of our efforts has to be for the benefit of the universe. If we try to seek God's support for converting a violent person, who has intentions of harming us, into a non-violent one; our efforts shall not remain selfless and then God's decision shall be independent of our efforts.

Gandhi was for right changes in human society and he was convinced that the right changes can be brought about only through right efforts made with right human intelligence.

Strong resolve to serve; total selflessness; intelligence aligned to universal intelligence; untiring and undaunted efforts; humility bringing ego level down to zero; intense **shraddha** in one's action and finally the sacred desire to offer the outcome of one's action to the God; that was the ideal action-plan of Gandhi to reduce pains and sorrows of human society. To those who think that it is an Utopian action-plan, I beg to submit that this kind of action-plan any mother makes in a fraction of second finding her small child in difficulty and implements it, in toto.

There is a proverb that says, 'As you sow so shall you reap'. Gandhi was firm on his views that right results can never be achieved with defective action or intent. It is difficult to understand Gandhi unless one finds some truth in the words of French philosopher Chardin, "*You are a spiritual being immersed in a human experience*". Most of us experience in our lives that things started and achieved with intent of harming others or the things that cause harm to others, ultimately harm the one who initiated and implemented them. In a big industrial town full of pollution one cannot see brilliantly shining stars at night but he can see them when he is in a natural setting. Similarly, in the modern world where much untruth and violence prevail, our minds also get clouded and we are not able to see serene beauty of truth and non-violence. This exactly is the reason why we are not able to understand that our thoughts and actions carry the intent with them. If the existing order is to be changed a two pronged strategy is essential. The strategy is to stop generating filth and to clean the existing filth. One cannot afford to use defective tools to repair a defect and produce something of good quality.

Some consider that that Gandhi's thoughts are too simplistic and outmoded because they bring in faith and religion under consideration more often than not. Harvard Gun Study (08.30.2013) appears to infer that reduction in number of guns does not necessarily reduce crimes and thereby appears to imply that laws are made for a moral and religious people. If spirituality, religion and faith have helped the humanity to sustain itself despite its history of wars and violence, it needs to be empowered; that was in Gandhi's mind. He even talked about empowering spirituality and faith by removing those violent aspects from them that might have been crept therein by their use by violent minds.

I consider that Gandhi made a big contribution to spiritual thought. He talked about eternal happiness through selfless service of humanity. It is about perfect selflessness. It implies that if one devotes himself selflessly to service of man (a creation of God) all his life in this real (material) world, then God will take care of him in the other world.

It is the 'participant-consciousness' I have spoken about earlier in this chapter. Spiritualists say 'this' world is an illusion. Realists say 'that' world is imaginary. Gandhi dispensed with the thought of 'illusion' and 'imagination' and seeded the thought of taking care of both the worlds. I am not saying that our scriptures had different intentions. Perhaps, the time and circumstances when our scriptures were conceived did not prompt our ancestors to emphasize this thought or may be those from modern times who are learned enough to interpret scriptures do not emphasize this thought for some reasons. Whatever may be the facts and circumstances, for us 'truth realized is as good as truth discovered'.

Although I have tried my level best to include all important and critical aspects of Gandhi's thoughts in his own words, still I wish to mention about something that he perhaps intended but did not specifically speak about. He took up the task of fighting against some of the practices in Hinduism, considered as a religion, which were not in accordance with accepted humanitarian norms. By doing so he not only served his own religion but also served other religions also. By attempting to clean his own religion he also became an example for others to initiate similar actions for their respective religions.

How do we serve humanity? We serve by taking actions that may empower human beings to do such things that help them to get rid of the problems they face. Gandhi fought against discrimination on the basis of colour of skin, he fought for independence of India, he fought against discrimination of people on the basis of castes, he fought for eradication of poverty and he also fought for improvements in many other social, political and economic conditions. None of his fights had any violence in them. He protested, refused to accept any unreasonable demand, opposed any act or gesture of the oppressor or the oppressed that he considered as violent. He inspired the oppressed for performance of their duties and for conducting themselves upholding truth and non-violence as ideals. He inspired by working with the oppressed bearing all hardships and taking all risks himself. He taught others what sticking to truth and non-violence is by becoming an example himself. Gandhi knew that like the oppressed oppressors were also human beings and like the oppressors oppressed were also human beings; both were good and both had many drawbacks. If oppressors do something good it must be appreciated and if possible repaid. If oppressed caused any harm that must be regretted and damage must be repaired. If one is fighting for a just cause justice must prevail. If one is fighting against violence non-violence must prevail. If we want to hear truth we cannot lie. We all have fear. We want to possess things and we hate losing them. If someone harms we want that he also suffers the way we are suffering. We want to satisfy our desires. We have pride and we want to win. If we are looking for a change where we have no fear, the only option is that we have no discrimination, no hate, no pride, no greed, no desires, no ill will, no enmity and above all, no fear.

If we want to take right action, we must fully understand what 'right' is. I have tried to discuss about many qualities viz. humility, self-respect, patience, absence of enmity and anger, *aparigraha*, *asteya*, sacrifice, penance, simplicity, self-discipline, forgiveness, compassion, courage etc. and of course, truth and non-violence. No one can claim that he can list all the good qualities, but all can draw big lists. Further, listing of right qualities is a fairly simple job but acquiring those qualities and moulding our conduct according to them, come what may, is a tough task. I can say that I have learned the quality of not being angry only when I have stopped being angry even in extreme circumstances; because only then I can help someone, whom I serve, to learn how to stop being angry.

While many think that they are unhappy because they do not have enough; Gandhi thought that one was not happy because he does not know how to be happy. He felt, saw, heard, experienced, read, thought, experimented and used the knowledge gained to solve problems, both internal and external. All this he did with great sincerity and commitment and he found that it worked. It worked defying all logics. He continued, made mistakes and learned more. Other joined him giving more opportunities to him with his experimenting. He learned about the strength of collective human efforts for exploring the golden principle of *'what is beneficial for all is right'*. He realized that most of the knowledge about what is right and what was wrong was already available but that was considered as too divine, holy and sacred to be handled by an ordinary human being in daily life. There is a proverb that says 'beauty is to be seen not to be touched'. Gandhi did not appreciate the idea of keeping divinity beyond the reach of man. Gandhi, consciously or subconsciously, felt that depriving man of opportunities to elevate himself is not right and produces results that are unwanted. If the man is prevented from 'touching beauty' he, who by nature loves beauty, starts playing with the beauty of swords and guns and detaches himself from the thought of *satyam shivam sundaram*.

Gandhi thought and said in no unclear words that man, by nature, is good and he has full rights to think and act for his good. Man lives in human societies and draws all kind of supports from them. He contributes to his physical environment and his physical environment nurtures him. This is true for all that is living or is inanimate. Changes do occur but slowly. Changes cannot and should not be forced. If sudden changes are forced they cause harm in all possible ways viz. physical, intellectual, emotional, spiritual etc. and then the man, circumstantially looses the right to think and act for his good. Gandhi's concept of 'immediate surroundings' is based on this phenomenon. To further clarify these issues I will take the case of India. About one thousand years ago India was invaded from north and could not defend itself. People from different cultures started ruling India for their physical comforts and convenience. They encroached upon the rights of an Indian man to do good to him. Undoubtedly, the invaders must have also harmed themselves in this process. Then about four hundred years ago British entered India for trading and subsequently started ruling it. The modern thought of 'individual freedom' and Gandhi's thought of 'self dependence' matched and got combined with economic and political weaknesses of British to make India free from British rule. Of course, those from a particular sect who thought that they were different from others living in India also separated from India. Did the matter end? Those powerful people living in this world who believed or just casually assumed that physical well being, comfort and materialistic growth is good enough for life; gained strength and invaded others with their capital, business, trade, commerce, language and culture. I add in this list of possessions of powerful people; 'tools for reduction of man's physical efforts for more profits'. People like Lenin and Nkrumah called it 'Neocolonialism' and those whose intellect is not aligned with universal intellect called it 'Globalization'. Capitalism cannot survive unless it expands its market. Globalization is an effort by rich countries to avoid their downfall and a compulsion for poor counties to remain dependent on rich countries. Gandhi's ideals of self-dependence were shelved by those who ruled India after its freedom; therefore India still remains dependent in many ways.

The thought that happiness can be achieved only through unbridled desire of materialistic achievements and growth, leads to selfishness; selfishness leads to causing harm to others; causing harm to others leads to fear; fear leads to worries; worries lead to impatience, urgency, pretentiousness, falsehood, theft, deceiving others and so on and so forth. This is violence.

God is always busy. He does not take any rest, not even a break; and keeps serving his creation day and night, but he has enormous patience and is an embodiment of peace. As against this the devil is always in a great hurry, much worried, agitated and is busy in crookedly strategizing and scheming to avoid his impending fall. If a few think that they can survive happily by making many others dependent on them, they are sadly mistaken. They should know that their violence is not being appreciated by many; that effectively means that they are not being liked by those on whom their survival depends.

Violence is not only cowardice but it also is foolishness of the highest order. The countries that are trying to expand their economic kingdom through their money power have already exported their culture, language, violent ideas and thoughts to the people whom they are trying to rule. The world is witnessing an incongruent marriage of violent interdependence of the exploiters and the exploited notwithstanding how many times one repeats the term 'mutual-dependence'. Violence in its extreme form does not spare anybody, not even the violent. It is suicidal. It is a pitiable situation. A man with good intentions will pity the powerful and also the weak. Unfortunately, the one who will suffer the most in this game is going to be the human being.

Gandhi could foresee all this. **He had clarified that when one serves his immediate surrounding and helps it to become self dependent, the distant surroundings are automatically served; as they get an opportunity**

to realize their mistake of depending on others for their good. Man can serve the universe only by realizing his limitations. When one disregards his immediate surroundings he serves none, neither the distant surroundings nor his immediate surroundings. He serves himself. Serving only oneself is theft and theft is also violence.

A farmer, who works hard in his field to grow food for himself and his family, takes care of his animals, sings with others in praise of God in evenings, and shares some food with the guests or those who are hungry is non-violent. We do find people like this farmer even today. There population is not insignificant. The universe is being well served by them. We, who read or write a book like this one, are not like him. Little introspection reveals that we are not untouched by violence. Our education and our livelihood compel us to get involved in violence. Our education makes us self-centered and good for use only to those who are not concerned about the humanity in its entirety. And the livelihood we earn comes from the principles of high productivity in depleting earth's resources, which we call as consumerism. Some exceptions may be there but they hardly matter because of their rarity. Sometimes we become a participant in violence, sometimes we help in promotion of violence and if we are too 'inert' we only observe violence holding prayers beads in our hand. We become liable to two kinds of offences in the court of humanity. First, of not paying off our debts that we owe to all those, living or dead, who have contributed for helping us live the way we are living;

and the second is of laying mines on the planet earth that will make life difficult for our future generations. Even if we leave aside the thought of God, religion, morality and ethics the question that still remains is whether despite our violence, we live a life of peace, contentedness and heartfelt happiness, fully realizing our worth as a human being?

I have generally not found people who lead a peaceful and happy life around me. I have generally found that today's man is not able to locate himself in the labyrinth of his existence. He is trapped in self-made cobweb, pushed by his intellect and pulled by his desires. The worst part is that he gives an impression that he does not have any faith in his ability to bring about any change in himself. Yes, it is true that generally a modern man, particularly if he is an educated one, either sticks to his one-sided vision or has an ostrich like disposition of burying one's face in sand to avoid danger. We often find that an amalgamation of selfishness and timidity awkwardly laced with false ego is the stuff very common these days. I must hasten to add that they are not the people who have buried their humanity too deep. It is only that they lack courage. Their education has miserably failed to make them aware of their true worth and realize how important they are for the world. But, there is also a very encouraging side of the picture. There are people in this world, of course, not in very large numbers, who have tried to view things objectively and honestly. These exceptional people have deep compassion, tremendous understanding and rock-like commitment for things that relate to humanity. They give us hope.

These people who can perhaps, changes the plight of human race appear to hover around either human **pravritti** or human **nivritti**. We have discussed about *pravritti*. *Nivritti* means orienting oneself towards deep contemplation about the life and beyond it and viewing that absolute truth and God are the only realities; and the material world that is short lived and destructible has nothing to offer to a human being except confusion.

This is a tragedy that the key findings of Gandhi's experiments have either remained little known or they were made known only marginally, clubbed with Gandhi's achievements that Gandhi himself never considered as his achievements. Gandhi did not appear to be very enthusiastic about happenings before and after the British gave charge of the country to Indians. No doubt, communal riots were one reason but that was not the only one; I am rather sure about it. To emphasize the point I intend to make, I quote hereunder from a speech that was delivered by Gandhi on 12th December, 1947 (this was also published in Harijan Sevak later) a portion of which has already been quoted in the relevant chapter.

> *I have no doubt that if we want to attain the independence which crores of Indian villagers begin to understand and feel, spinning on spinning wheels and wearing Khadi has to become more important than*

*ever . . . . Through Khadi we were trying
to ensure that instead of electricity driven
or steam driven machines riding on man,
the man stays above them. Through Khadi
we were trying to ensure that the difference
between man and man, of rich and poor, of
higher up and lowly that we see today is
eliminated and instead of it we are able to
establish equality between man and man,
and also between man and woman . . . .
What we were trying to do in last thirty
years that was not moving backwards. We
must continue with activities related to
spinning wheel and other allied activities
with better understanding and with more
vigour.*

(Harijan Sevak; 12.21.1947)

*I am spending my time in service of the
people. I am unable to view selfless
service as mere work to achieve some
results . . . . My efforts towards leading
life cannot be divided into different
compartments. At the root is the same old
thing, call it truth or non-violence.*

**(From the speech in New Delhi on
09.22.1947)**

Spinning wheel for Gandhi was symbol of self-dependence of billions of human beings through which they could have earned their livelihood by using their bodies, intellect and soul. Spinning wheel for Gandhi was a resolve for human dignity by not letting anyone use human beings as means of production in his selfish interests. Spinning wheel was a non-violent answer by Gandhi to demolish the violence perpetrated by the British on traditional Indian textile industry for the benefit of their textile mills in Manchester. Spinning wheel for Gandhi was a well thought plan backed by 30 million people from a country that grew cotton in plenty, to counter Neocolonialism that was written on the walls.

It is unlikely that I could have thought exactly the way Gandhi thought; in fact it could have been the result of *Yoga* that silently emerges in support of a selfless action by human being. The true outcome of Gandhi's experiments with truth and non-violence had the potential of staging a live demonstration of self dependence by a sizable population of people who were forced into poverty by violent intentions and violent means. The exemplary part of this self dependence would have been its realization; that would have kept human dignity and non-violence at the centre of all human endeavours.

Did Gandhi ever say that he wanted the world should move backwards? All he intended was to warn those who were planning to copy others without thinking of ground realities and with no consideration for building a strong self-reliant base for India that did not encroach upon the legitimate rights of others. If one says that 'machines are for man' and not the other way round; what is wrong with it? Gandhi always said that Charkha was a symbol. No one knows by whom and in which century it was invented. Gangabehn Majumdar, a widow, found it in Vijapur in the state of Baroda in India and Gandhi's team made it workable for millions. It was bread and butter for many. It still is. It is almost a century now! Our education system has not been able to produce a single student who could use his intellect to produce a 'machine' that gives food to one without snatching a *roti* from the plate of another human being. [*Roti* is a kind of bread eaten by Indians.] Those who think that Gandhi wanted to reverse the wheel of man's progress, in fact, have no confidence in human intellect that it can feed all without leaving at least some hungry.

The outcome of Gandhi's experiments with truth and non-violence was the knowledge of creating silent revolutions along with the wisdom that the humanity has to be at the centre of everything. Like self-dependence, self-control and self-rule Gandhi's concept of revolution was **'Self-revolution'** or **'Aatm-Kranti'**. Here, *aatm* means what is related to self, soul or spirit and *kranti* means revolution. A flow diagram is given on page 331 titled as 'Gandhi's Perpetual Action' to show pictorially as to how, according to my imagination, Gandhi would have normally worked. This would help the readers to easily understand what we have been discussing and what we may discuss hereafter.

When one brings about necessary changes in him to be able to connect himself with others through selfless service and thereby helps those whom he serves, to bring about necessary changes in them to serve many more selflessly and this goes on and on; *aatm-kranti* is initiated. It is needless to say that selfless service is impossible without adhering to truth and non-violence and the both are silent expressions of divine love that is automatically experienced by the *sadhaks*. The word 'silent' in silent revolution has a deep meaning. This silence is the real strength of such revolution and can be achieved by courageous and unwavering commitment that is possible through the qualities of *penance* and *patience*. This real strength appears due to inexplicable scientific reasons and silently empowers the action. It is *yoga*. It is decisive physical strength generated from unseen and unknown sources and the *sadhak* wins.

GANDHI'S PERPETUAL ACTION

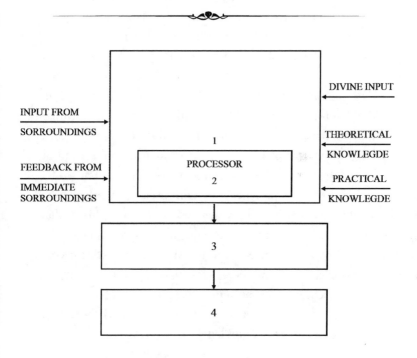

1. Perfect Selflessness and Humility for Input, Output & Processing

2. All Output must conform to Truth & Non-Violence

3. Sthitprajna State

4. Immediate Surroundings to be Serviced

This *yoga* is realized when *pravritti* does not obstruct *nivritti* and *nivritti* does not come in the way of *pravritti.*

When worldly duties are according to universal intelligence, that is they are governed by what is truth and do not envisage any harm to the lowliest in the universe, they become **Dharma**. One has to have a fierce commitment for **Dharma**; for which *satvik* penance, sacrifices and patience are necessary. This part is of commitment towards and performances of one's exalted duties (**Dharma**). During this part the *seeker* remains in the realm of *pravrittis*. When in the process of performing his **Dharma** he becomes detached to losses or gains, happiness or sorrow, praise or criticism, reputation or defamation; and when pleasures or comforts do not attract him, when he experiences no pains from all the losses he might have incurred and when he has no fear of losses that he may have to incur or the pains he may be subjected to; he attains a state of equanimity. He becomes **sthitprajna** and the revolution silently occurs. By this revolution human beings gain, the humanity gains and above all the seeker gains tremendously; and he knows it! Ultimately it becomes a universal knowledge.

INTERNAL REVOLUTION (AATM-KRANTI) IS NOT IMPOSSIBLE

We human beings by nature are compassionate. Compassion is an emotion that may best be responded to by making an active, and if possible, a decisive contribution in dealing with the cause of misery of others. If I see a poor family in a miserable state due to hunger and make a creative film on the family so that others can also feel the way I have felt, my action and my film shall be nothing but representative of a callous human society; unless I intend to make an appeal to the viewers to do something for dealing with the miseries of the poor family. Can there be a best way of responding to the misery of others? Let us generalize this question and ask; can there be a best way of responding to our miseries?

Since time immemorial man has moved ahead along with others trying to live better than the previous day. I do not know to what extent human instincts and human intelligence contributed in formation of human societies. I am however sure that man has realized that if individuals largely submit to their self interests and take less care of others, the process of degeneration in societies begins. God made men with almost equal abilities but not exactly equal abilities. Men with lesser abilities would grow lesser food than those with more abilities. Such differences would never be large and would automatically be taken care of by the good qualities man possesses of compassion, benevolence and kindheartedness. Further, if I am in trouble today for any reasons and you help me, it does not mean that both of us would continue with our respective conditions for ever. Tomorrow I may be required to help you. In this process both of us live happily making use of our good qualities. When we say that God did not make us equal, we actually refer to this natural phenomenon of co-existence of good and evil. It is the difference between 'equal' and 'almost equal'. It is the difference between 'ideal' and 'practical' or difference between 'theory' and 'practice'. It is a phenomenon that we accept and never say that existence of evil negates the divine goodness that the God represents. The problem does not lie here.

The problem started when some in the state of temporary abundance of physical nature, be it possession of natural resources or the ability of acquiring natural resources, started discriminating others who did not enjoy that abundance; and also started a process of maintaining the status-quo. Few of us having something more than others started creating and maintaining a new order of difference between man and man to become more secure than others. No doubt to provide relief to those who became less secure in this process, man made efforts to restore God's order by conceptualizing principles and practices of religions and morality. These principles helped us but always fell short of our needs. Any effort against God's order is violence. Violence can be perpetrated through missiles and bombs, 'isms' and theories, cooked-up statistics and propaganda, religions and peace talks or whatever means one can use to ensure that injustice prevails. Man's intellect had always been more aligned to material. More physical security, more materialistic possessions for comfort, more opportunities for satisfying sensory desires etc. have always attracted the man. Religions and principles of morality have never superseded man's desires and violence.

Violence is not an evil because it harms others. Violence is an evil because it harms. If we are a part of system that is violent we are violent. But today we are not only a part of a violent system; we have become a participant therein.

Think of anything you are surrounded by; a bathing soap, a pack of chocolates, packaged food, a medicine, your refrigerator, your car, a religious conference, an educational institute, a multinational company you work with or an international organization for human welfare; you will find violence. Perhaps it would be better idea to make a visit to a wildlife sanctuary to learn what non-violence is.

Those who believe in rebirth would agree that we will have to pay the price of our sins of today; and those who do not believe in rebirth would agree that our descendants will have to pay the price of our sins of today. We are an honourable species of the planet earth. If we do not solve our problems, then who will?

We cannot be made to dance like an animal in a circus for a bowl of stale rice at the end of the day or a bundle of dollars at the end of the month. If we dance like an animal, we do it out of fear that something would definitely go wrong with our bowl of rice or bundle of dollars.

Courage is the answer for fear. Courage is a quality that is not dormant in those who are courageous. Gandhi developed his theory after much experimentation. We have discussed his theory earlier in this chapter when we dealt with the concept of *Aatm-Kranti*. Gandhi made it very simple when he suggested that one should serve only according to his ability, neither less nor more. He made it simpler by suggesting that one should serve his immediate surroundings only. Lastly, he also gave importance to patience. Any action to change our condition will definitely call for sacrifices on our part. We are fearful of making sacrifices. That is the cause of our lack of courage. When Gandhi said that one should do what he can do and he should go about everything patiently; he presumed that there existed a strong will to do. Anyone who possesses the quality of compassion can develop a will to change the plight of many, and that 'many' must necessarily include him. When we develop qualities necessary for serving others selflessly, the quality of summoning enough courage for making sacrifices automatically gets enhanced within us. No doubt, at least in initial stages our desires and intellect may allow us to make only small sacrifices. It is not important to make a big sacrifice; what is important that one sticks to do what he has pledged. The biggest hurdle in the path would be to realize true selflessness, for which one who serves always remains the sole judge. This greatly enhances the ability of introspection and helps in several ways.

It is of paramount importance to understand that when we decide to rise and do something about ourselves, we would be required to do three things together. One, we would be trying to become a true man or true human being. Two, we would be trying to help others in becoming true human beings by making ourselves an example before them. Three, our goal in the entire exercise would be to demolish some violence somewhere without resorting to violence of any type on our part. A little thinking would suggest all the three above complement one another and make a forward movement possible.

We all can change 'our life' to remind us that we are human beings and thereby giving meaning to our individual lives. That was Gandhi's equanimous realization as a revolutionary. Gandhi knew that if we moved five miles on the path of truth and non-violence; for ourselves, for the fellow human being and for the God; the God will push us forward by ten miles.

Gandhi's thoughts remind me of the intellect working behind Hubble Space Telescope. If you cannot view the cosmos very clearly due to atmospheric distortions of light; why break your head in making more and more powerful telescopes sticking to earth? Why not go beyond the earth in an orbit and see the cosmos from there? It seems that the space scientists told themselves that the cosmos and earth were not two separate entities and rising above the earth to become a part of cosmos was the solution.

What happens when we see beyond ourselves and serve the 'universal self' that is beyond us, but not too far away; that is what Gandhi experimented with. He found it works in favour of humanity. The world observed that impact of his work was many times greater than what could have been possible by efforts put in by a man of fragile body from a slave country pitted against the most powerful of his times. What more is expected from a human being? I clearly see a finger pointed toward the world and questioning, "Why Gandhi's work was not continued?"